TIME

Einstein

The Enduring Legacy of a Modern Genius

TIME

MANAGING EDITOR Richard Stengel
DESIGN DIRECTOR D.W. Pine
DIRECTOR OF PHOTOGRAPHY Kira Pollack

Albert Einstein: The Enduring Legacy of a Modern Genius

WRITER/EDITOR Richard Lacayo
DESIGNER Arthur Hochstein
PHOTO EDITOR Dot McMahon
RESEARCHER Kathleen Brady
COPY EDITOR Barbara Collier
EDITORIAL PRODUCTION Lionel P. Vargas

TIME HOME ENTERTAINMENT
PUBLISHER Richard Fraiman
GENERAL MANAGER Steven Sandonato
EXECUTIVE DIRECTOR, MARKETING SERVICES Carol Pittard
EXECUTIVE DIRECTOR, RETAIL AND SPECIAL SALES Tom Mifsud
EXECUTIVE DIRECTOR, NEW PRODUCT DEVELOPMENT Peter Harper
DIRECTOR, BOOKAZINE DEVELOPMENT AND MARKETING Laura Adam
PUBLISHING DIRECTOR, BRAND MARKETING Joy Butts
ASSISTANT GENERAL COUNSEL Helen Wan
BOOK PRODUCTION MANAGER Suzanne Janso
DESIGN AND PREPRESS MANAGER Anne-Michelle Gallero
BRAND MANAGER Michela Wilde
ASSOCIATE PREPRESS MANAGER Alex Voznesenskiy

SPECIAL THANKS TO:
Christine Austin, Jeremy Biloon, Glenn Buonocore, Malati Chavali, Jim Childs, Susan Chodakiewicz, Rose Cirrincione, Jacqueline Fitzgerald, Christine Font, Lauren Hall, Carrie Hertan, Malena Jones, Mona Li, Robert Marasco, Kimberly Marshall, Amy Migliaccio, Nina Mistry, Dave Rozzelle, Ilene Schreider, Adriana Tierno, Jonathan White, Vanessa Wu, TIME Imaging

ISBN 10: 1-60320-173-4
ISBN 13: 978-1-60320-173-5
Library of Congress Number: 2010941157

We welcome your comments and suggestions about TIME Books. Please write to us at:
TIME Books, Attention: Book Editors, P.O. Box 11016, Des Moines, IA 50336-1016

If you would like to order any of our hardcover Collector's Edition books, please call us at 1-800-327-6388, Monday through Friday, 7 a.m. to 8 p.m., or Saturday, 7 a.m. to 6 p.m. Central Time.

Contents

Mr. Universe

Albert Einstein's immense breakthroughs in theoretical physics revolutionized our view of the cosmos and made him one of the towering figures of the 20th century, a man whose name is synonymous with genius

By RICHARD LACAYO

I N 1999, AS THE 20TH CENTURY drew to a close, it seemed an obvious moment to ask, What person had the greatest impact on the past 100 years? Or, as a special issue of TIME published at the end of that year would put it, who was the Person of the Century? Was it Winston Churchill? Franklin D. Roosevelt? Mahatma Gandhi? Nelson Mandela? All those worthy candidates were considered for the cover of that issue. But in the end, they had merely changed the world. There was one man who had changed the universe.

Before Albert Einstein, that universe was presumed to behave according to rules first arrived at in the 17th century by Sir Isaac Newton that could almost be called commonsensical. Einstein suspected that nature's rule book was a far stranger affair. In 1905, when he was just 26 years old and working as an obscure technical expert in a Swiss patent office, he developed a startling new picture of reality. In Einstein's universe, space and time were not absolute and unchanging but "relative"—things that could stretch or shrink depending on the observer. And from that realization, he drew a further conclusion: that matter and energy were two aspects of the same thing and could emerge from each other. He expressed that understanding in the most famous scientific formula of all time: $E = mc^2$. With that short but momentous string of letters and symbols, he opened the door to the atomic age.

As audacious as the special theory of relativity was, Einstein had more to offer. In 1915 he completed work on the general theory of relativity, which provided an entirely new model of gravity. Instead of being a force of attraction that all objects exert upon one another, which was the view dating back to Newton, Einstein declared that it was a bending in the elastic fabric of "space-time." As the renowned British physicist Sir Stephen Hawking would write in TIME's Person of the Century special issue, Einstein's discovery that space and time are warped was "the greatest change in our perception of the arena in which we live since Euclid wrote his *Elements* about 300 B.C."

After British scientists confirmed Einstein's startling new theory in 1919, he suddenly became one of the most famous people in the world. His rumpled clothes and ragged mop of hair would become as familiar as the mustache and bowler hat of Charlie Chaplin's Tramp. Yet he would never become puffed up, never play the regal genius. He *was* a genius, of course, but he behaved in public like a lovable uncle.

Einstein even resisted attempts to make his discoveries seem more broadly important than they already were. He was impatient with the interpretations of relativity that made it symbolize the cultural upheavals of the early 20th century that we call modernism. Yet almost a century later, we can't help but see his willingness to dynamite centuries-old scientific beliefs as being in some way a product of the same climate that produced Picasso, Stravinsky and James Joyce. If the heavens themselves were in an uproar, why not fracture pictorial space, bend harmony and take a hammer to the novel? By describing a universe that operated in such unexpected ways, relativity could make it seem as though God himself had given a permission slip to revolution.

However strange it may seem, the uncanny picture of the universe offered by Einstein's theory of relativity has been confirmed again and again. Now that high precision instruments such as atomic clocks and lasers are available to test his ideas, they have shown that he was absolutely on target with the equations he worked out with nothing more than a pencil.

The Times of London *announces confirmation of general relativity*

And almost half a century after his death, scientists are still confirming some of Einstein's predictions about what they would find as they look deeper into the workings of nature. Gravity lenses, dark energy, black holes and the Big Bang were all things foreseen by Einstein's theories, though sometimes he was reluctant to believe them himself. Even the theoretical quest that seemed most quixotic during his lifetime has attracted new interest. For decades Einstein attempted to develop a unified field theory, a model of the universe that would explain gravity and electromagnetism as manifestations of a single force, connecting the movement of planets and stars with the operations of the tiniest subatomic particles. It was an undertaking that yielded no answers while he lived. But today the quest for a "theory of everything" has been taken up again by physicists struggling with what's called "string theory." In that theory, the tiniest particles are actually parts of a string that can vibrate at different registers, causing them to act as different particles, somewhat the way a violin string can sound as an A or B, depending on how it's tuned.

Is it just a coincidence that Einstein loved to play the violin? Perhaps he was on to something even there.

THE CONQUERING HERO
On his first trip to the U.S., in 1921, Einstein is given an official motorcade through the streets of New York City

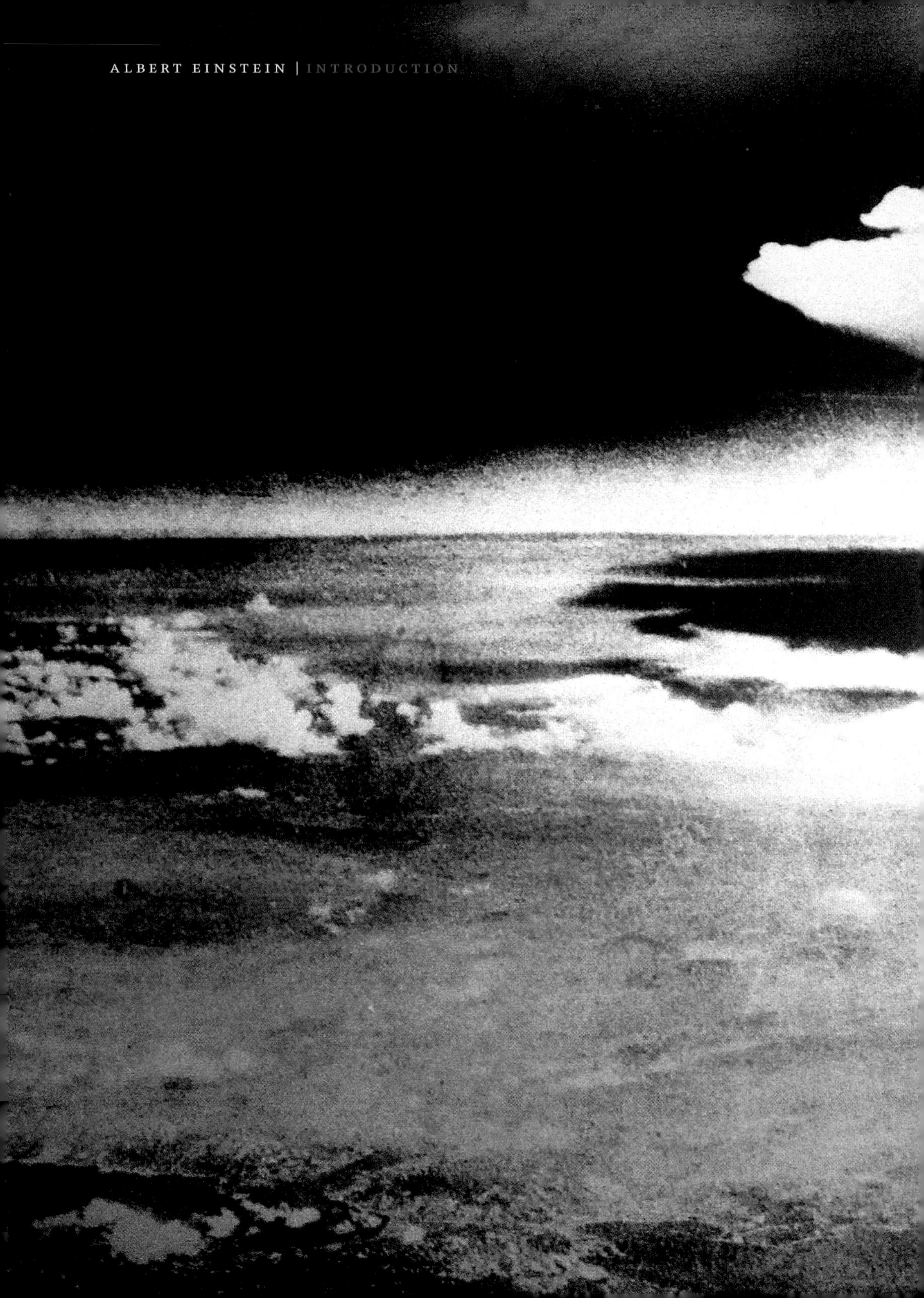

THE FRUITS OF HIS LABOR
Einstein did not work on the development of the atomic bomb, but his discovery of the equivalence of mass and energy made it possible

THE FINAL FRONTIER
*The general theory of relativity not
only explained gravity in a new way,
it also opened up a window on the
origins of the universe*

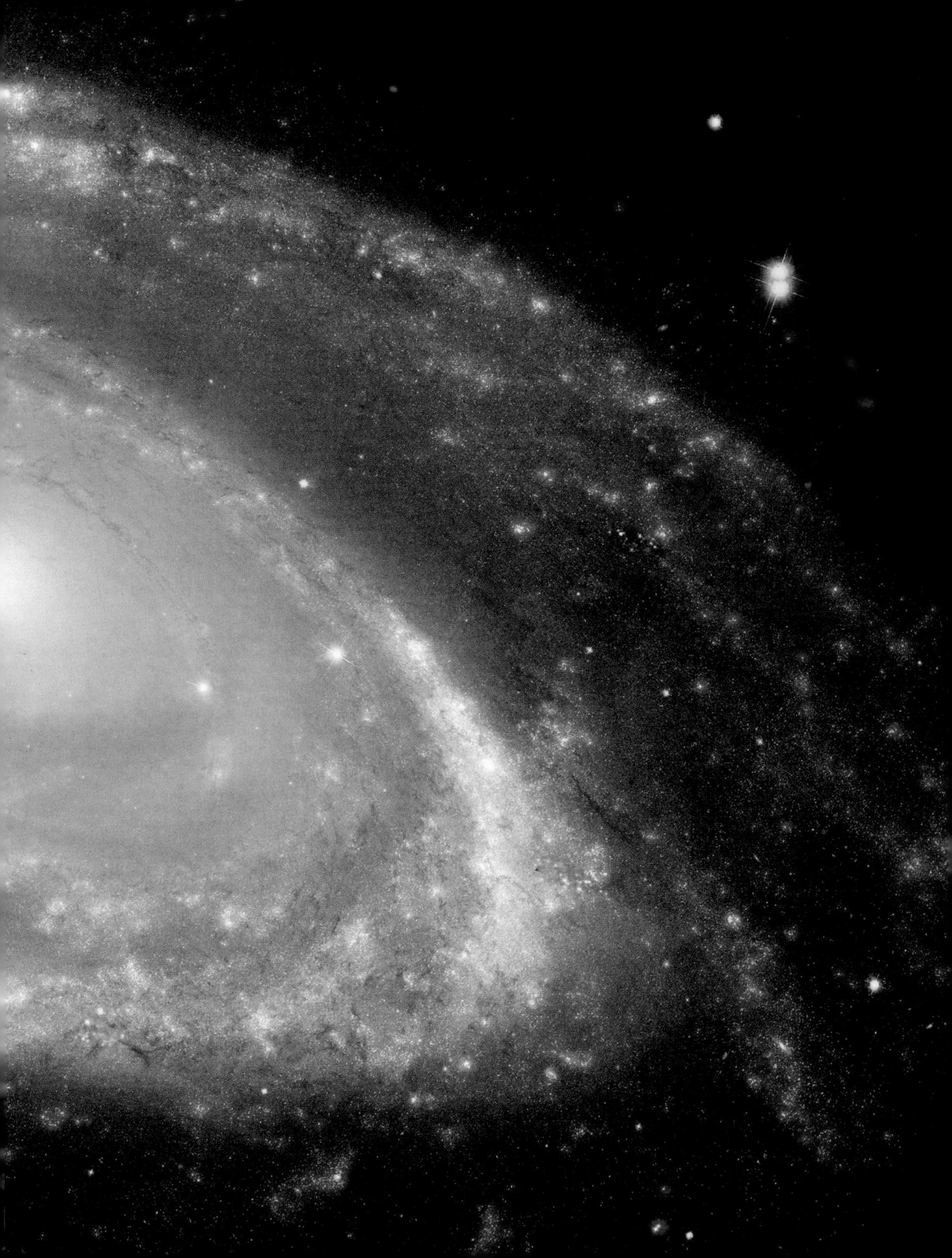

His Life

1879
Born in Ulm, Germany, on March 14. His family moves to Munich the following year

1881
Sister Maria, known as Maja, is born

1896
On his second attempt, passes entry exam for Zurich Polytechnic

1900
Gets diploma from Polytechnic

1901
Becomes Swiss citizen

1902
His daughter Lieserl is born out of wedlock to his future wife Mileva Marić

1906
Receives doctorate from University of Zurich

1910
Birth of son Eduard

1911
Becomes professor at German University in Prague

1919
Divorces Mileva. Marries Elsa

British scientists confirm general theory through observation of a solar eclipse. Einstein instantly becomes world famous

1921
First visit to U.S. to raise funds for the Hebrew University

1928
Continues work on unified field theory, great preoccupation of his later life, while recuperating from serious heart problems

1930
Debates quantum mechanics for the second time with Niels Bohr at the Solvay Conference. Makes second trip to the U.S. to take temporary post at Caltech

1932
Accepts position with new Institute for Advanced Study in Princeton, N.J.

1939
Signs letter to Franklin Roosevelt urging research into atomic bomb

1940
Becomes an American citizen

1946
Named chai of Emergenc Committee of Atomic Scientists

1894

Leaves high school before graduating to join family in Italy

1895

Enrolls at school in Aarau, Switzerland. Lives with family of Jost Winteler

1903

Weds Mileva; they move to Bern. Lieserl presumably is given up for adoption

1904

Hired by Swiss patent office as Technical Expert Third Class. His son Hans Albert is born

1905

His miracle year: publishes a string of groundbreaking scientific papers, including those on light quanta and the special theory of relativity

1912

Made professor at Zurich Polytechnic. On a visit to Berlin, becomes reacquainted with his cousin Elsa

1914

Becomes professor at University of Berlin. Mileva walks out, taking their sons

1915

Completes the general theory of relativity

1922

Wins 1921 Nobel in Physics. Tours Asia and Palestine

1925

Co-discovers Bose-Einstein condensate

1933

Hitler takes power in Germany. Einstein's summer house in Caputh is raided by Nazis. He relocates to U.S.

1936

His wife Elsa dies

1952

Offered presidency of Israel by Prime Minister David Ben-Gurion but declines

1955

Dies from a ruptured aneurysm. His ashes are scattered along the Delaware River. His brain is preserved for medical research

CHAPTER 1

Birth of A Beautiful Mind

O N THE DAY ALBERT EINSTEIN came into the world—March 14, 1879—in the small city of Ulm in southwestern Germany, he did not bear the stamp of genius in any obvious way. But he did emerge with a stamp of sorts. His head was oddly misshapen, with an enlarged occipital bone in the back. His parents even feared that his appearance might be a sign of mental impairment. There was no need to worry. For the most part, his skull would soon normalize, though for the rest of his life, the back of his head would be notably square shaped. And no one would ever accuse him of being mentally insufficient.

BOY WONDER
Einstein at three. He took so long to learn how to talk that a family maid called him the "dopey one"

Albert's parents, Hermann and Pauline, were German Jews with long roots in Swabia, the region where Ulm, an ancient city on the Danube, is located. Albert was their first child. There would be just one more, a sister Maria, called Maja. Born two years later, she would become one of her brother's greatest friends and confidants.

At the time of Albert's birth, Hermann was a partner in a featherbed business. But very soon it failed. Luckily, his brother Jakob, an engineer, had his own gas and electrical supply company in Munich, which Hermann was invited to join. Gladly accepting, he moved his family to a Munich suburb, where Albert would spend his childhood in a comfortable home with a garden.

Family legend has it that Albert did not speak until relatively late, perhaps not before the age of three. For a time he also developed a fierce temper and a tendency to fling things during tantrums. He was five when he threw a chair at a woman who was tutoring him at home. She ran off and never returned. On another occasion he hurled a wooden bowling ball at his sister's head. Maja would later recall the incident wryly: "It takes a sound skull to be the sister of an intellectual."

At around the same age that he chased off his tutor, Einstein had what he would later recall as a profoundly affecting first recognition of the mysteries of the physical world. Sick at home one day and confined to his bed, he received from his father the gift of a compass. Watching the compass needle spin in obedience to the invisible force of magnetism, he became thrillingly aware that, as he would later put it, "something deeply hidden had to be behind things."

It was also during his preschool years that his mother gave him entrée to another world of order, this one not so hidden. She arranged for him to learn the violin, the beginning of a life-long joy in music, especially Mozart's. Later he would also take up the piano. As an adult, Einstein would often reach for his violin when he was engrossed in a difficult problem in physics. Like Sherlock Holmes, he found that playing helped him think through challenging puzzles.

At six, he was ready for school. The only private Jewish academy in Munich had closed in 1872 because it had failed to attract enough students—a sign, perhaps, of how eager the city's Jewish population, about 2% of the whole, was to assimilate. Thus, Einstein's parents sent him to a large Catholic school. As resolutely nonobservant Jews, they would have been untroubled by the school's church affiliation. But as the only Jew among 70 second-grade pupils—the level at which young Einstein entered, thanks to his years of preschool tutoring—their son got an early taste at school of anti-Semitism, through insults and even physical assaults. "For the most part not too vicious," he later recalled. "But they were sufficient to consolidate even in a child a lively sense of being an outsider."

At school, Einstein continued to be, as he had been at home, somewhat isolated from children his own age. He also chafed at the rigorous discipline of a German school, even on the elementary level. Looking back years later, he would say, "The teachers at the elementary school seemed to me like drill sergeants and the teachers at the high school like lieutenants."

Einstein moved to that high school, Munich's Luitpold Gymnasium, at the age of nine. Despite persistent legends that as a boy he did poorly in his studies, it would be truer to say that in subjects that interested him, notably science and math, he excelled. But even with disciplines that left him cold, like Latin and Greek, he performed adequately. In high school he also underwent a brief but powerful episode of religious fervor, discovering with great excitement the God of the Old Testament and his prophets. The 12-year-old Einstein began to keep kosher and composed hymns to God's greatness that he sang to himself as he walked to school. Under

THE LAUNCH PAD
The apartment building in Ulm where Einstein was born; Ulm, below, a Swabian city nestled along the Danube, as it looked around 1895

the guidance of a rabbi, he began preparations for his Bar Mitzvah—the ceremony by which a boy becomes a full member of the Jewish community following his 13th birthday.

Einstein's moment of religious ecstasy was cut short by his deepening investigations into natural science. In that area, he was especially in the debt of a medical student, Max Talmud, who came into his life when he was 10. Einstein's parents began inviting Talmud into their home every Thursday for lunch, in keeping with the Jewish tradition of providing a regular meal for a poor scholar. As gifts for their precocious son, he often brought with him books of popular science, including the 21 illustrated volumes of a series called *People's Books on Natural Science*. As Einstein later described it, his early reading convinced him "that a lot in the Bible stories could not be true. The result was downright fanatical freethinking, combined with the impression that young people were being deliberately lied to by the state ... it was a shattering discovery." The plans for a Bar Mitzvah were dropped. More than that, something in Einstein's whole outlook was changed by his repudiation of scriptural religion. "From this experience," he wrote later, "grew a mistrust of any kind of authority. A skeptical approach to the convictions which were current in whatever social environment I found myself—an attitude which never left me [though] it subsequently lost something of its original edge."

Just as his doubts about religion were mounting, Einstein found a new obsession—mathematics. His friend Talmud brought him a book about planar geometry—the "sacred little geometry book," as Einstein would call it. From there he moved quickly on his own into analytical geometry and calculus, realms of higher mathematics where even Talmud could no longer follow. But Einstein's deepening fascination with mathematics did not translate into an easier time at school. He found the authoritarian methods there ever less congenial. His growing dissatisfaction was brought to a head by a change in his family's circumstances. In 1893 the firm headed by his father and his uncle lost an important contract to electrify Munich's center city. With insufficient work elsewhere in Germany, Hermann and his brother Jakob decided the next year to relocate their operations to Italy, near several small projects of theirs. Hermann moved his family to Milan, then to Pavia, about 20 miles to the southeast, where the Einstein company was building a new factory. But it was decided that 15-year-old Albert would remain in Munich, living in a boardinghouse until he finished high school.

The prospect of three years of solitary life and boardinghouse accommodations made the boy miserable. He knew that if he remained in Germany, he also faced compulsory military service after graduation, a possibility he dreaded. Without telling his parents, Einstein took it upon himself to seek a discharge from school on grounds of "neurasthenic exhaustion." By Christmas he was reunited with his somewhat startled family in Pavia.

Einstein was happy to be out of Germany and loved the culture and people of Italy, even as he recoiled at Pavia's "uniformly filthy walls and streets." His father, however, was not so pleased that his son was now a high school dropout with no prospects and only vague ambitions to teach philosophy. Hermann pushed his dreamy boy to obtain some kind of technical degree. Einstein at last agreed to apply to the Zurich Polytechnic. A highly regarded school, it had the additional advantage that a high school diploma was not a requirement for admission. Einstein would merely have to pass an entrance exam. Confident of his abilities, he set himself to a course of private study to prepare for the test.

As it turned out, he was too confident. He failed, largely because of gaps in his knowledge of French, chemistry and biology. But his examiners were sufficiently impressed by his predictable mastery of math and physics that the school's principal proposed that he enroll for a year at

FAMILY AND FRIENDS
Clockwise from top left: Einstein's father Hermann; Einstein and his sister Maja, about 1885; his mother Pauline; a smiling Einstein, in the front row, third from right, with mostly unsmiling classmates, in Munich in 1889

VOYAGER OF THE MIND
Einstein, in a Munich photo studio, at age 14

a nearby high school, brush up on the topics he was weak in, then take the exam again.

To Einstein's surprise, the forward-looking school in Aarau, Switzerland, about 30 miles from Zurich, had a very different atmosphere from the authoritarian school in Munich. Its curriculum and faculty emphasized "free action and personal responsibility" in a way that delighted him. So did the family he boarded with in Aarau. Jost Winteler taught history, Greek and Latin at the Aarau school. He and his wife Pauline had seven children, and their household provided Einstein with an instant surrogate family.

The Wintelers may have been important to young Einstein in another way. Jost Winteler was deeply concerned about the growth of militarism in Germany, especially after Prussia's victory over France in the Franco-Prussian War of 1870-71. Einstein was already receptive to those concerns, but Winteler's views may have influenced him to take a decisive step. In January 1896,

THE RIGHT PLACE
Einstein, seated at left, with classmates at Aarau, which he much preferred to rigid German schools

Einstein renounced his German citizenship. (He soon applied for Swiss.) In the document casting off his citizenship, which was filled out by his father, he also appears to discard his identity as a Jew—or to try to. He describes himself as being of "no religious denomination."

One of the Winteler children, their 18-year-old daughter Marie, also became the 16-year-old Einstein's first romantic infatuation. After studying to be a teacher, she was living at home while she awaited her first posting. She and Einstein would go bird-watching and play music together. When he went back to Pavia for spring break, they exchanged frequent letters. In one of them he told her, "You mean more to my soul than the whole world did before."

All the same, this would turn out to be no more than a brief teenage romance. In the fall of 1896, after passing the entrance exam for the Polytechnic on his second attempt, Einstein returned to Zurich to start school. Marie moved to a teaching post not far from her home. By the following spring, he had decided to break off the relationship. He had met someone new. She was Mileva Marić, the only woman among the 23 students in Einstein's program at the Polytechnic, which offered teacher training in math, physics and astronomy. He remained close to the Wintelers, however, and his sister Maja would one day marry Maria's brother Paul.

The daughter of a prosperous Serbian family of farmer-

OVER AND OUT
Einstein's last Aarau report card—high grades in math and science, but just a "3" in French

FUTURE ORIENTED
*Einstein in 1896, the year
he entered the Zurich
Polytechnic*

landowners, Marić was three years older than Einstein. Whereas Einstein was considered good looking and sensuous in his youth, Marić was plain and walked with a limp, the result of a congenital hip defect. But she had other qualities that were far more important to Einstein. She was a true intellectual companion, a woman who could share his passion for physics and math, someone with whom he could explore books and ideas. By the fall of 1897 their relationship had become sufficiently intense that Marić felt it necessary to withdraw temporarily from the Polytechnic and audit classes at Heidelberg University, which did not formally admit women. But throughout the months she spent there, she exchanged flirtatious letters with Einstein in which he urged her to return to Zurich. The following spring, she did.

In June 1900, Einstein would graduate from the Polytechnic, a very unspectacular fourth in his class of five. As for Marić, her final grades were too low for her to graduate at all, so she decided to repeat her last year and take the diploma exam again. Einstein spent an uneasy summer vacationing in Switzerland with his parents, who were fond of Maria Winteler and deeply unhappy about his newly announced intention to marry Marić. And all the while there was an even more pressing challenge than bringing his parents around—he needed to find a job.

Though he fully expected to get one as an assistant instructor at the Polytechnic, Einstein soon discovered that both of the physics

ONE PLUS ONE EQUALS TWO
A student at the Polytechnic, Mileva Marić shared Einstein's passion for science and mathematics

professors there regarded him as more arrogant than brilliant and wanted nothing to do with him. While he and Marić scraped by in Zurich offering private lessons, Einstein burnished his résumé by drawing up a theoretical paper that attempted to explain capillary action—the way, for instance, that a liquid rises up a narrow glass tube. Though the explanation he proposed would turn out to be misguided—he later called it "worthless"—the paper became his first published work. In March 1901 it appeared in the *Annalen der Physik,* the most prestigious European journal of physics. The following year he succeeded in publishing a second paper in the *Annalen* that was concerned with the same molecular forces of attraction. But when he proposed to pursue his interest in those forces as the topic of a doctoral thesis at the University of Zurich, the idea was rejected.

Throughout 1901, Einstein engaged in an ever more desperate pursuit of a position, without success. Then in March he got word from a friend that a job would be opening soon for a clerkship at the Swiss patent office in Bern. It wasn't a place in academia, and it would be months before the job would materialize, but the prospect excited Einstein all the same. Living once more back with his parents in Italy, he wrote to Marić in Zurich: "Just think what a wonderful job this would be for me! I'll be mad with joy if something should come of that."

CHAPTER 2

A Time for Discovery

W HILE HE WAITED TO learn whether there would be a job for him at the patent office, Einstein took a temporary teaching post at a school in Winterthur. In February 1901, Einstein had become a Swiss citizen, though he would be excused from compulsory Swiss military service because of varicose veins and flat feet. Before starting the teaching job, he decided to take a romantic vacation with Marić on Lake Como in Switzerland. Very romantic, as it turned out. Einstein later wrote to her about "how beautiful it was [when] you let me press your dear little person against

PAIR OF HEARTS
*Einstein with Mileva a few
years after their wedding*

FOR WHOM THE BELL TOLLS
Bern's historic clock tower would
help inspire the theory of relativity

me in that most natural way." Nature took its course, and soon after their trip, Marić found herself pregnant. In his next letter to her, after rhapsodizing on a "wonderful paper by Lenard on the generation of cathode rays by ultraviolet light," he got around to asking his pregnant lover: "How's the boy?"

Actually, it would be a girl that Marić gave birth to in January 1902 at her parents' home in Novi Sad, a Serb city in what was then part of Hungary. She was named Lieserl. A few weeks later, with his teaching job at Winterthur completed—as well as a disagreeable stint at a private school in Schaffhausen—Einstein moved to Bern, where the patent office had finally advertised the job opening he hoped to fill. Marić remained with her parents while she recuperated from a difficult labor. As they made plans to embark on a life together, the circumstances of the young couple were not promising. When he arrived in Bern, Einstein was still not assured that the clerkship was his. And though Marić had retaken her diploma exam at the Polytechnic the previous summer, once again she had failed, ending her hopes for an academic career in physics. Meanwhile, Einstein's mother Pauline was still fiercely opposed to the prospect of their marriage. Shortly before Lieserl was born, Pauline even sent a bitter letter to Marić's parents, accusing their daughter of deliberately seducing her son.

MEETING OF THE MINDS
Einstein, at right, with the members of his Olympia Academy, Conrad Habicht, left, and Maurice Solovine

Waiting for the patent office to act, Einstein took a cheap furnished apartment not far from Bern's famous clock tower and privately tutored a few students to make ends meet. With one of them, Maurice Solovine, he quickly decided to put aside the tutoring relationship and instead invited him to drop by each week to discuss physics and philosophy over simple meals of sausage, cheese, fruit and tea. Soon they were joined by Conrad Habicht, a math student whom Einstein knew from the Zurich Polytechnic. The trio became lifelong friends and called their little group the Olympia Academy. Though the name was meant in jest, they applied themselves very seriously to philosophical works by Plato, John Stuart Mill and David Hume and to the scientific inquiries of Ernst Mach.

At last, in the spring the patent office came to the rescue with a job offer that Einstein eagerly accepted. On June 23 he began work as a Technical Expert Third Class, with an annual salary of 3,500 Swiss francs—almost twice what he would have made as an entry-level assistant professor in academia. His chief duty at the office would be to decide whether an invention submitted by a patent seeker was indeed new or whether it infringed on already existing patents. Sometimes, on the basis of drawings and specifications, he would also have to decide whether the thing actually worked.

At a moment when the field of electrical devices was booming, and when cities all around Europe and the U.S. were rushing to electrify, it was particularly useful for the patent office to have someone with Einstein's background as a physicist who understood electromagnetic phenomena. For his part, Einstein quite enjoyed the work. As he described it to a friend, "it is enormously varied and calls for much thought." But not so much that he could not often finish the day's tasks in the morning, leaving himself the remaining hours to focus on his independent scientific pursuits.

In October 1902, Einstein's father, just 55 years old, died at home in Milan of heart failure. On his deathbed, with Albert in attendance, the elder Einstein at last gave his son permission to marry Marić. With her husband gone, Paulina left Italy, returning to Germany to live with a sister. Einstein's sister Maja returned to school in Aarau. Einstein returned to Bern, where a few months later, Marić joined him—but not with their child. Lieserl was left in the care of Marić's parents, possibly because Einstein's job would have been jeopardized were it known that he had fathered a child out of wedlock. On January 6, 1903, he and Mileva were at last wed in a civil ceremony at the Bern registrar's office. No family members attended. The witnesses were Einstein's friends from his Olympia Academy.

In the end, Lieserl would never be sent for. The fate of Einstein's first child is one of the great mysteries of his life story. Most biographers believe she was put up for adoption in 1903 and that Einstein never set eyes on her at all. We do know that in August of that year, Mileva journeyed back to Novi Sad temporarily because Lieserl had contracted scarlet fever. Soon after, a cryptic letter from Einstein to Mileva asks, "How is Lieserl registered? We must take great care, lest difficulties arise for the child in the future." It's a passage that may imply that Einstein wished to be sure that the girl's birth papers were in order at the time of her adoption.

After he became famous, Einstein never made public that he and Mileva had conceived a child before their marriage. Lieserl would remain a family secret until decades after his death. Not until 1986 did the correspondence between Einstein and Mileva mentioning the girl come to light. In that year a cache of letters—retrieved from Mileva's apartment after her death in 1948 and brought to California by the first wife of Einstein's son Hans Albert—was discovered in a safe deposit box where Hans Albert's second wife had later stored them.

It was observed by some who knew Mileva that when she rejoined Einstein in Bern, she had a melancholy air about her. Could she have been saddened by the decision to give up her daughter? Whatever the reason, by the autumn of 1903 she and her husband had moved to a new apartment, and she was pregnant again. On May 14, 1904, she gave birth to a boy, Hans Albert, an event that apparently lifted her spirits. Einstein, too, was delighted and became a doting father, doing things like fashioning a toy cable car for his little son from a matchbox and string. Years later a friend described stopping by for a visit to the Einsteins in their cramped apartment and coming upon the new father: "With one hand, he was stoically rocking a bassinet in which there was a child. In his mouth, Einstein had a bad, a very bad cigar and, in the other hand, an open book. The stove was smoking horribly."

That same year the multitasking Einstein was also at work on a challenging project, a third scientific paper, this one on the molecular theory of heat. In that paper he took an important step toward developing the idea, first put forward by the German physicist Max Planck, that light consisted of discrete bundles of energy—quanta. And in doing so he opened the way to one of the revolutionary breakthroughs he would make in the series of hugely important papers he would publish in 1905. In that year, in the space of just a few months, the obscure patent clerk in Bern would utterly transform not just the science of physics but the entire 20th century world. Still just 25 years old, Einstein was on the threshold of his *annus mirabilis*—the "miracle year."

How the Universe Worked— Before Einstein

For a long time, Newton's laws of physics seemed to describe things well—until the discovery of electromagnetism demanded some serious rethinking

To understand the revolution brought about by Einstein in his miracle year of 1905, it's important to grasp just how scientists understood the workings of the universe before he came along. The best place to start is in the 17th century with Sir Isaac Newton. The great English physicist had his own miracle year, in 1666, when as a 23-year-old university graduate, Newton developed a theory of color, arrived at his main ideas about gravity and motion, and invented calculus, the new form of mathematics he needed to complete his descriptions of space and the forces that act upon objects within it.

Building upon ideas first put forward in the 16th century by Galileo, Newton developed three famous laws of motion. The first states that unless it is acted upon by an outside force, an object in motion will continue to travel in a straight line at uniform speed. The second law holds that when a force is applied to an object in motion, the object will accelerate at a rate proportional to the force. And the third declares that every force

applied to an object produces an equal and opposite force.

Applying his new laws to the motion of heavenly bodies, Newton recognized that a planet in orbit around the sun moves in its elliptical path, instead of shooting straight out into space, as a consequence of some force being applied to it. That force is the one we call gravity, which Newton further realized was the same force that caused an apple to fall to the ground. He would later tell a friend that it was the sight of an apple dropping from a tree that led him to the insights that culminated in what we now call his "universal law of gravitation."

In essence, that law states that a force of attraction works among all objects in the universe so that everything pulls at everything else, from the tiniest atoms to the most immense stars. With any two bodies, the strength of that force is proportional to the mass of each and varies inversely as the square of the distance between them. According to Newton, if you know the mass of an object and calculate the forces acting

SIR ISAAC NEWTON
The great 17th century physicist told friends that he began to formulate his famous theory of gravity after he observed an apple falling from a tree

upon it, you can chart its movements with confidence, whether the object is a rock flung through the air, a comet whizzing through space—or that fateful apple.

Fundamental to Newton's picture of the universe was the idea of "absolute" time and space. In his cosmos, a minute on Earth is of the same duration as a minute on the moon or Venus. Likewise, a yardstick on Earth is of the same length as a yardstick anywhere in the universe. And the movement of any object can always be measured against these absolutes. But these apparent certainties are things that Einstein's theory of relativity, with its notions of "relative" time and space that are different for different observers, would utterly explode.

All the same, because they worked so well in most ordinary circumstances, Newton's laws would endure for two centuries as one of the two great foundations of physics. The second emerged in the 19th century and was still evolving when Einstein was a student. This was the theory of electromagnetism. Its most profound advances were made by a Scottish scientist, James Clerk Maxwell, working at King's College in London in the 1860s. Whereas Newton's universe was based on forces, Maxwell described a universe governed by more complex fields.

And what is a field? A sort of bristling, active space. An electric field, for instance, describes the continuum of distorted space around an electrically charged object. Likewise, a magnetic field describes the properties of the space around a magnet. Place a bar magnet beneath a piece of paper that's been sprinkled with iron filings, and you can see that field for yourself. The filings will arrange themselves on the paper in curved paths emanating from both ends of the magnet. That complex web work is the magnetic field. And as Einstein himself would describe it: "It is not the charges nor the particles, but the field in the space between the charges and the particles, that is essential for the description of physical phenomena."

Maxwell was not the first to delve into these questions. In the 1820s scientists had shown that an electrical current run through a metal bar could produce magnetism. Soon after, the self-taught English scientist Michael Faraday, one of Einstein's great idols, proved that a changing magnetic field could, in turn, produce an electric current. And how do you produce a changing magnetic field? One way is simply to move a magnet toward or away from a metal coil. The approach or withdrawal of the magnetic field

will cause the coil to produce an electric current.

By applying his discoveries, Faraday went on to invent the electric generator. In the 1860s, Maxwell came along to develop an elegant set of mathematical equations to describe these electromagnetic fields. In so doing, he demonstrated that not only would a changing magnetic field produce a changing electrical field but also that a changing electrical field would produce a changing magnetic field—and that further, the magnetic field would produce another electrical field, which would, in turn, produce another magnetic field, and so on endlessly, with the interlocking fields becoming a single expanding electromagnetic field.

With that, Maxwell mapped out a whole model of electromagnetism, one that would lead in time to the invention of things like radio broadcasts and cell-phone transmissions. He also showed that these electromagnetic fields move at the speed of light through space as waves. In fact, as Maxwell was the first to declare, visible light is itself one of these electromagnetic waves.

Maxwell's discoveries were so revolutionary that for years they were ignored in the physics departments of most universities. When Einstein entered the Zurich Polytechnic in 1895, he was aware of Maxwell's findings, which he described as "the most fascinating subject at the time I was a student." But to his great disappointment, his professors stuck to teaching the classical physics of Newton.

Yet the challenge of electromagnetism would prove hard to avoid. It was leading to problems for the science of physics generally, because Newton's mechanics and Maxwell's electromagnetism contradicted each other in some ways. For one thing, Newton believed his forces, like gravity, propagated themselves through space instantaneously, at infinite speed. But Maxwell's waves moved over time (though very quickly—at the speed of light.) And if Maxwell was correct that light was a wave, a question arose: When it traveled through space, in just what substance was it waving? He decided that the substance was a stationary gas called "aether" and that it filled the universe, though no scientific instruments had ever detected it anywhere. If anything, experiments suggested there was no such thing.

So it was that by the early 20th century science had built a beautiful edifice of laws to describe the operations of the universe, but the universe insisted on breaking them. It was at this point that Einstein arrived, pen in hand, to rewrite the laws in fundamental ways.

JAMES CLERK MAXWELL
The 19th century Scottish physicist arrived at the equations that describe the phenomenon of electromagnetism, of which visible light is one example

CHAPTER 3

The Year
He Shook
The World

I N THE SPRING OF 1905, THE YEAR EIN-
stein would produce his phenomenal string of scientific papers in a condensed burst of genius, he
sent a letter to his Olympia Academy friend Conrad
Habicht, who had moved from Bern. Einstein play-
fully taunted Habicht, who had recently completed his dissertation, to send it along: "Don't you know that I am one of the
1½ fellows who would treat it with interest and pleasure, you
wretched man?" In return, Einstein promised to send Habicht
four papers he had recently worked on. "The first deals with radiation and the energy properties of light," he explained, add-
ing the tantalizing promise that it was "very revolutionary."

EXPERT THIRD CLASS
Einstein in 1905, when he was a 26-year-old patent-office clerk

Einstein, who was not a man to throw around the word revolutionary, was not overstating the case. So challenging to conventional science was his first paper of that year, completed in March, that when he published it later in the *Annalen der Physik,* he titled it a "heuristic viewpoint" on light. Heuristic? It's a word to describe a hypothesis that provides a useful way to think about a problem but that itself may not be proved or even provable. Knowing very well how powerful his new idea was, Einstein was bringing it out into the world on tiptoe.

That paper laid the foundation for a new understanding of the basic question: What is light? Did it consist of particles, as Sir Isaac Newton had surmised, or was it a wave, as most scientists in the first years of the 20th century had come to believe? Einstein would determine that it could be regarded not only as a wave but also as a series of particles. His conclusion rested upon a hugely significant departure from classical physics undertaken a few years earlier by the great German physicist Max Planck. In 1900, while attempting to explain the properties of radiation, Planck had decided that matter could be said to emit and absorb light not in continuous waves but in discrete bundles. He would call these tiny packets quanta, because each contained a particular quantity of energy. But Planck thought of his quanta merely as a mathematical device necessary to explain the behavior of light when it interacted with matter, as with radiation. He could not believe they described an intrinsic property of light itself.

It fell to Einstein to make that conceptual leap. Applying Planck's quantum theory to explain what's called the photoelectric effect—the way some metals give off electrons when light falls on them—he declared that those bundles were not simply a feature of how light was absorbed or emitted. They were rather the very thing that light consisted of, even when it flowed through a vacuum, a place where there was no matter to interact with. We now call those bundles "photons." In the 1920s they became the basis for the development of quantum mechanics, the field of physics that describes the behavior of subatomic particles and regards light—indeed, all matter—as something that can have the properties of both a particle and a wave.

It was for that discovery that Einstein would be awarded the 1921 Nobel Prize in Physics. Yet the quantum was so radical a departure from classical physics that he harbored doubts about it until the last years of his life, by which time the rest of the scientific world had long since accepted the idea. And as the years went by, the emergence of quantum mechanics as the accepted explanation for the behavior of subatomic particles would greatly disturb him.

Einstein's next paper, which he completed in April and which involved determining the size of sugar molecules in water, did not revolutionize the world of science. But when he submitted it that summer to the University of Zurich as his doctoral dissertation, it did at last earn him his long sought Ph.D.

In his third paper, which he produced in May, little more than a week after completing the second, Einstein returned to the question of atoms and molecules in a much larger way. In this case he established with authority that they existed, something doubted by many physicists at the time. Einstein arrived at that proof in the course of explaining the phenomenon of Brownian motion—the jiggling, darting movement of small particles suspended in water. Brownian motion was named for the Scottish botanist Robert Brown, who first observed it in 1828 when he was using a powerful microscope to examine grains of pollen in water. What caused that strange movement? Some scientists speculated that it was the result of invisible molecules of water colliding with the floating particles. Einstein's leap forward was twofold. First, he proved that water molecules randomly colliding with the particles could indeed move them in those odd patterns. He also produced a formula that made it possible to determine the number of molecules within a given volume of liquid or gas—in other words, a way to measure molecules.

However important the papers on light quanta and Brownian motion were for the world of science, it was his last two papers of 1905 that made Einstein the towering figure he is for everyone today. Thomas Edison famously said that genius is 1% inspiration and 99% perspiration. We don't know what ratio of those factors went into Einstein's momentous discovery of relativity, but we know that both were involved. His conceptual breakthroughs arrived only after much strenuous and often frustrating study and calculation in the little apartment at Kramgasse 49 (a place you can still visit today). But there were also apparently some moments of pure inspiration.

Einstein awoke early one morning in May in great excitement, feeling as though, as he later put it, "a storm broke loose in my mind." For a long time he had been preoccupied by the problem of the speed of light. When he was 16 years old, he used to imagine running alongside a beam of light, wondering what he would see. If he were running at the same speed as the beam, would it appear to be stationary, the way a car riding alongside your car at the same speed appears to be standing still? But by 1905, Einstein had learned that in Maxwell's equations, light always traveled at the same speed. No matter how fast an observer might also be traveling, he or she could never catch up. Even as that observer herself approached the speed of light—186,000 miles per second—a beam of light would still appear to dash away from her at the speed of light. How could that be?

THINK TANK
The restored two-room apartment at Kramgasse 49 where Einstein worked on some of his groundbreaking papers

As he struggled with that paradox in the spring of 1905, Einstein began using an old friend, Michele Besso, as a sounding board for his speculations. Six years older, Besso was a companion from Einstein's student days in Zurich who had come to work with him at the patent office. He was also married to a sister of Marie Winteler, Einstein's first love interest. Einstein was in such despair at one point that he told Besso he was going to give up on the problem. But on a crucial afternoon in May, while in conversation with Besso, a key turned within his mind. The next day Einstein called on his friend. Before even bothering to say hello, he abruptly declared, "Thank you. I've completely solved the problem."

One catalyst for that brainstorm was something he had done the previous night—he rode in a streetcar past Bern's famous clock tower. It was something he had done many times before. But as he glided past the clock that night, the familiar confluence of motion and time somehow helped bring him face-to-face with a strange realization—there is no "absolute time" of the kind presumed by Newton's physics, in which time is the same everywhere. Instead, time and space are different for different observers, depending on how fast they are traveling. The faster you go, the more time slows down. And as you approach the speed of light, space would distort as well. Things would appear to shorten. Though Newtonian physics might be fine for understanding the world of our everyday experience, when you move toward a world of lightspeed, things are very different. As for the "aether" that was supposed to fill the universe and supply a universally valid means to measure a state of rest—the aether scientists had sought in vain for years to detect—it was time, Einstein realized, to stop chasing that figment. There was no such thing, and further, it wasn't needed as a way to understand the cosmos. And with that Einstein—who was still a 26-year-old clerk in the patent office in Bern—applied a giant eraser to generations of scientific thinking and put in its place a profound new picture of the universe.

Inspiration having done its job, it was time for perspiration again. Over the next few weeks Einstein worked feverishly to commit his new insights to paper, eventually covering 31 handwritten pages to produce "On the Electrodynamics of Moving Bodies." But in its completed form, though its ideas were utterly groundbreaking, the language of his paper was anything but laborious. In his biography *Einstein: His Life and Universe,* Walter Isaacson calls Einstein's momentous treatise "one of the most spunky and enjoyable papers in all of science. Most of its insights are conveyed in words and vivid thought experiments, rather than in complex equations." No scientific predecessors were credited by Einstein either, though there was a note of thanks to his friend Besso.

EINSTEIN'S SPECIAL THEORY OF RELATIVITY

Relativity asserts that light moves through a vacuum at a constant speed relative to any observer and no matter what the observer's motion. From these claims follow bizarre consequences that challenge common sense and our customary perception of reality—but have been verified repeatedly by experiments.

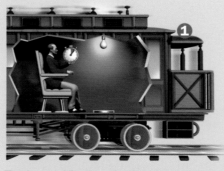

The observer riding the train thinks the lightbulb and the mirror are standing still

RELATIVITY AND TIME

A moving clock runs slower than a stationary one from the perspective of a stationary observer.

1 A man riding a moving train is timing a light beam that travels from ceiling to floor and back again. From his point of view, the light moves straight down and straight up.

2 Watching from trackside, Einstein sees the man, the bulb and the mirror moving sideways; the light traces a diagonal path as it goes. From Einstein's viewpoint, the light travels farther. But since the speed of light is always the same, the same event measured on his clock takes more time.

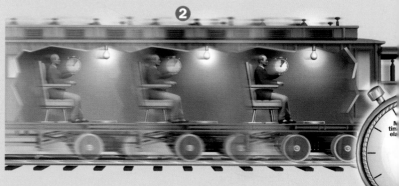

The observer watching the train thinks the lightbulb and the mirror are moving

Graphics by Ed Gabel

Sources: *World Book Encyclopedia; Einstein for Beginners*

Einstein mailed off the manuscript to the *Annalen* in June, then took to his bed for days in a state of utter exhaustion. Meanwhile, Mileva, well trained in mathematics, applied herself to checking the majestic assertions in her husband's paper. A few weeks later, with both their energies restored, husband and wife went out to celebrate, as confirmed by a comical postcard they sent to their friend Habicht: "Both of us, alas, dead drunk under the table."

Soon enough he would get up from under the table—his miracle year was not over yet. There would be one more astounding insight, which he presented in a three-page paper that he published in the *Annalen* in November as a "mathematical footnote" to his paper on relativity. In it he said that his relativity principle had led him to conclude that "the mass of a body is a measure of its energy content." Indeed, matter could become energy and energy become matter. And even the tiniest speck of matter might be able to release a phenomenal amount of energy.

Einstein summarized this insight in what is now the most widely recognized scientific formula of all time, the one almost everyone knows. Even if few of us truly comprehend it, we grasp its tremendous power because it unleashed the atomic age. Energy, he proclaimed, equals mass times the square of the speed of light.

Or to put it more famously: $E = mc^2$.

RELATIVITY AND LENGTH

A moving object appears to shrink in the direction of motion, as seen by a stationary observer.

1 The man now observes a light beam that travels the length of the train car. Knowing the speed of light and the travel time of the light beam, he can calculate the length of the train.

The observer watching the train sees only the motion of the light beam

2 Because Einstein is not moving with the train, from his point of reference, the rear of the train will be moving forward to meet the beam of light, making the light beam appear to be shorter. Because the speed of light is always the same, he will calculate the train's length to be shorter. Part of this effect is offset by the fact that his clock is moving faster, but part remains: the train actually shrinks. As the train approaches the speed of light, its length shrinks to nearly zero.

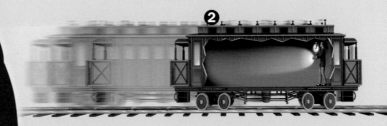

Someone watching from outside sees the light beam moving, but with the motion of the train added

CHAPTER 4

"Newton, Forgive Me"

EINSTEIN HAD SET OFF AN EX-
plosion in the house of physics. Indeed,
three of his seminal 1905 papers, including
the first relativity paper, had appeared in a
single issue of the *Annalen*. But it took time
for the ripples from that explosion to move outward within the
scientific community and for other physicists to arrive at a response, or rather a range of responses, to the challenging revi-
sions he had put before them.

So revolutionary were his ideas on light quanta that even
scientists who recognized his genius were reluctant to accept
his conclusions. Max Planck, the pre-eminent theoretical

TIME AND SPACE EXPLORER
Einstein in 1905, the year he produced the special theory of relativity

physicist in Europe, soon opened an admiring correspondence with Einstein. But even Planck, the first to propose quanta as a means of thinking about the absorption or emission of light, remained for a long time unwilling to think of them as something that light actually consisted of. All the same, Planck helped legitimize relativity through a lecture he gave in Berlin and an article he published in the spring of 1906. He also sent his assistant Max Laue to visit with Einstein in Bern. After arriving at the patent office, Laue was so unimpressed by the disheveled person who entered the waiting room looking for him that he assumed it could not possibly be Einstein. Only when Einstein went back to his office and then re-emerged did Laue realize that this unimposing figure was the man who had rewritten the laws of physics.

And was still rewriting them. In 1906, Einstein somehow found time to produce six additional papers, including several that further explored his new equation $E = mc^2$, as well as his theories of Brownian motion and light quanta. With Planck's blessing, other physicists and mathematicians also began taking up relativity, confirming and extending Einstein's discoveries. It helped Einstein sustain his remarkable productivity that, though he had been promoted to the post of Technical Expert Second Class, with an annual raise of 1,000 Swiss francs, his work at the patent office was still not terribly demanding, leaving him time to pursue his theorizing there. One visitor recalled Einstein opening one of his desk drawers and announcing that this was his department of theoretical physics.

Over the next couple of years, an attempt to translate his immense gifts as a theorist into profitable new inventions would lead him to develop and patent an electrical device for laboratories that he worked on with his friend Conrad Habicht and Habicht's brother Paul. But in the end, that project came to nothing. Einstein was no Edison. And let it be said, Edison, who was never a theorist, was no Einstein.

No matter, even as his attempt to become an inventor was faltering, Einstein's growing prominence in the world of physics had renewed his hopes of pursuing an academic career. As a step toward that goal, in the spring of 1907 he applied to the University of Bern to become a *privatdozent,* a campus lecturer, whose income was derived from admission fees paid by anyone who chose to attend his talks. With his application, Einstein submitted 17 of his published papers, including the ones on light quanta and relativity. But he was turned down because the university refused to waive a rule that applicants also had to submit one unpublished paper.

By that year Einstein was also embarked on what would be his next momentous intellectual achievement. It grew out of problems he began to examine when he was asked to prepare an article on relativity for the *Yearbook of Radioactivity and Electronics.* His attempt to sketch out a comprehensive account of his theory brought him face-to-face with two shortcomings. It applied only to imaginary "inertial systems," in which things moved at a uniform constant speed in relation to one another. In the real universe, things were constantly accelerating and slowing down. And it did not accommodate the laws of gravity as developed by Newton. In particular, Newton believed gravity propagated itself instantaneously through space, but in relativity theory, the speed of light was the fastest possible velocity, and gravity would have to move through space over a period of time governed by that limitation.

As Einstein turned these problems over in his mind, he had another of his sudden bursts of inspiration, which he later described as "the happiest thought of my life." It happened in November 1907. "I was sitting in a chair at the patent office in Bern when all of a sudden a thought occurred to me: If a person falls freely, he will not feel his own weight." Over the next eight years, this insight would lead him to the general theory of relativity, yet another profound new picture of reality—this time one that introduced the startling notion of curved space and opened a window onto the birth of the universe itself.

Why was this insight about weightlessness important? Because it led him to realize that gravity was indistinguishable from accelerated motion and that their effects were both produced by, as he said, "one and the same structure." To put it another way, to someone standing in a rocket ship, unless he could look outside to see if his ship was moving through space or sitting on the launchpad, it would be impossible to tell whether his legs were being pulled downward by gravity or being held to the floor because he was accelerating upward. He would feel the same pressure in either situation. Likewise, in both environments, a dropped ball would fall in exactly the same way.

In time, this realization of the equivalence of acceleration and gravity led Einstein to the discovery that gravity was not a "force," as Newton had described it, but

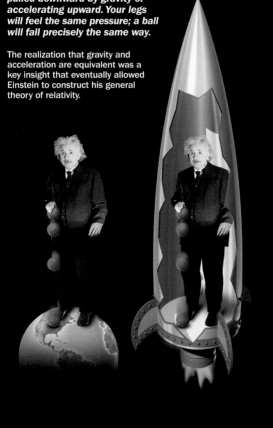

The Equivalence Of Gravity and Acceleration

Without external clues, it's impossible to tell if you're being pulled downward by gravity or accelerating upward. Your legs will feel the same pressure; a ball will fall precisely the same way.

The realization that gravity and acceleration are equivalent was a key insight that eventually allowed Einstein to construct his general theory of relativity.

the result of a warping of the fabric of "space-time," a bending that was caused by the movement of matter through space. In the final version of his article for the *Yearbook,* he was already able to apply and extend his equivalence idea to show that gravity could even bend rays of light. But it would take him eight years to work out all the implications of his discovery.

Meanwhile, he still needed to make a living. By the summer of 1908, Einstein had at last succeeded in obtaining a position as a *privatdozent* at the University of Bern by agreeing to write the additional paper required of all applicants. But by that time he was also being considered for a newly created associate professorship in theoretical physics at the University of Zurich, the same prestigious school that had granted his doctorate. He would be offered the job in March

AT THE BIG TABLE
*Einstein, second from right, at the first Solvay Conference for Europe's scientific elite, in 1911.
Seated with her head resting on her hand is Marie Curie, the pioneer of radioactivity*

1909, despite the fact that some faculty members had serious qualms about his disorganized lectures and disheveled appearance. In his book *Einstein's Cosmos,* Michio Kaku quotes the recollections of a student who attended Einstein's first lecture: "He appeared in class in somewhat shabby attire, wearing pants that were too short and carrying with him a slip of paper the size of a visiting card on which he had sketched his lecture notes."

The move to Zurich, accompanied by Mileva and their son, set off an incident that would lead Einstein to an important shift in attitude toward his wife. His appointment at the university was announced in a newspaper item that caught the eye of a young housewife in Basel. Anna Meyer-Schmid had met Einstein 10 years earlier at a resort hotel, when she was a girl of 17 and he was a 20-year-old vacationing with his mother. At one point, the ardent young man wrote a poem in the girl's album: "What should I inscribe for you here?/ I could think of many things/ Including a kiss/ On your tiny little mouth."

Now, a decade later, Meyer-Schmid sent Einstein a postcard congratulating him on his new position. He sent back a mildly flirtatious reply. Though he mentioned that he was married, he suggested that if she ever got to Zurich, she should look him up—and he gave her his office address, not the one for his home. Anna responded with another note—one that Mileva intercepted and interpreted as flirtatious in its own way. Outraged, she wrote a letter to Meyer-Schmid's husband claiming that Einstein was offended by the suggestive letter. Einstein was compelled to send the husband another letter apologizing for Mileva's "extreme jealousy." It all blew over, but the episode changed Einstein's view of his wife and her dark moods. Though by the end of that year Mileva would be pregnant again—she gave birth the following July to their second son, Eduard—their marriage was on increasingly shaky ground.

Even as Einstein's personal life was proving difficult, his professional life was flourishing. In September 1909 he delivered a pivotal lecture to a scientific conference in Salzburg, in which

KISSING COUSINS
Einstein and his second wife, his cousin Elsa, embarking on their first trip to the U.S., in 1921

for the first time, he clearly enunciated a seemingly bizarre conclusion that his 1905 paper on light quanta appeared to compel—that light could be a continuous wave and yet also a stream of particles. By now his eminence within the field of physics was such that just months after assuming his new role as an assistant professor in Zurich, he was offered a professorship—at twice his Zurich salary—at the University of Prague. After some delay, caused by the reluctance of people in the Austrian ministry of education to offer the distinguished post to a candidate of Jewish ancestry, Einstein was approved for the job.

So by March 1911 he and his family were in Prague, stopping along the way to visit for the first time with one of his intellectual heroes, the Dutch physicist Hendrik Lorentz, who would become a close friend. In October he traveled to Brussels to be a key speaker at the first of several Solvay Conferences that he would attend over the years. Funded by the Belgian industrialist Ernest Solvay, they were periodic meetings of Europe's top physicists, a scientific elite of which the 32-year-old Einstein was now a respected member. Soon after, Einstein, having barely touched down in Prague, was offered a 10-year appointment as a professor at his former school, the Zurich Polytechnic, which had recently become a university, the Swiss Federal Institute of Technology.

By that time Einstein would be deeply engrossed in the further development of his new ideas about gravity, the concepts that would become the general theory of relativity. To describe in mathematical terms the warped space-time his theory required, he set out to master a form of geometry pioneered in the 19th century by Carl Friedrich Gauss and further developed by his student Bernhard Riemann, one that offered tools for investigating curved surfaces. Using devices like "Riemann tensors," he could set out the immensely complicated universe in which, as Einstein biographer Albrecht Folsing describes it, "the distribution of matter determines the curvature of space and hence the paths of material bodies, whose movement in turn changes the curvature of space."

All the while, his home life continued to suffer. Mileva was miserable in Prague and also somewhat envious of her husband's success. This was the state of affairs in the spring of 1912, when Einstein traveled alone to Berlin, where he reconnected for the first time since childhood with a cousin, Elsa Löwenthal, recently divorced and living with her two daughters. She and Einstein were cousins on both sides of the family. Her mother was the sister of Einstein's mother. And her father was a first cousin of Einstein's father. Like Mileva, she was three years older than Einstein, but she was otherwise very different—carefully groomed, consummately bourgeois, with a lively disposition and a livelier sense of social position, especially her own.

LITTLE EINSTEINS
Eduard and Hans Albert in Switzerland in 1919

Einstein was smitten. So was Löwenthal. On his return to Prague, he would receive a letter from her suggesting that they set up a secret correspondence through his office address. In short order, he sent letters to her proclaiming that "I have to have someone to love. Otherwise life is miserable. And this someone is you." Beset, however, by doubts, he wrote two subsequent letters insisting that they break off their long-distance romance. Which they did—for a while.

By that summer, Einstein and his family were back in Zurich and delighted to be there. They could now afford a six-room apartment with fine views. But Mileva's dark moods persisted. The onset of a new affliction—painful rheumatism—did nothing to help. And by May 1913, Löwenthal had come back into the picture by way of a birthday letter to Einstein that was also a plain invitation to renew their acquaintance. Soon he was telling her that he would like to come to Berlin to see her.

A few months later, an opportunity presented itself. Max Planck and another prominent German scientist, Walther Nernst, came to Zurich to entice Einstein to relocate yet again, this time to the University of Berlin. They promised he would have no burdensome teaching duties and would also enjoy a well-paid position in the Prussian Academy of Sciences and be made the head of a new physics institute. Despite his long-held distaste for the strict German temperament, within hours he accepted their offer. Almost at once he sent off an excited letter to Elsa, exclaiming, "I already rejoice at the wonderful times we will spend together."

By April 1914 the Einsteins had relocated. He settled easily into his new academic post in Berlin, though the perenially disheveled genius chafed at the urgings of his fellow academicians that he dress with greater care. But Mileva detested the German capital. As a Slav, she felt herself despised by the Germans. To make matters worse, she was now living not far from Einstein's mother, who still disliked Mileva intensely. And she and Einstein were increasingly estranged. Just two months after arriving, Mileva went back to Zurich. She took the children with her, a blow that devastated Einstein. The boys would never live with their father again.

Einstein agreed to give Mileva and the children half his salary for their support. He also moved out of the apartment they had barely inhabited together and took one closer to Löwenthal. Longing to see his children, he managed to make one brief visit to Zurich in 1915. There was another the following Easter, which did not go well. By that time Hans Albert increasingly sided with his mother. On that visit Einstein attempted to get Mileva, who still hoped for a reconciliation, to agree to a divorce. For whatever reason, she immediately became seriously ill. When she recovered a few weeks later, a daunted Einstein informed her that he would no longer press for a divorce, which appeared to mollify her. In the summer of 1917 he also managed to repair his relationship with Hans Albert while they traveled together to a sanatorium in Switzerland to drop off Hans' sickly brother Eduard, who suffered from a lung inflammation.

Through all the tumult in his personal life, Einstein was devoting what he would describe as "positively superhuman efforts" to his new theory of gravity. By May 1913 he had readied the paper that would present his general theory of relativity in its first form. It was produced in collaboration with an old friend from his student days at the Zurich Polytechnic, Marcel Grossman. Now a mathematician, it was he who had first pointed Einstein to the Riemann equations that proved so crucial to his efforts. But once it appeared, the paper confounded many of the physicists who read it. Though his special theory of relativity had largely won over the profession, Einstein was not widely supported at first in his attempts to produce an entirely new picture of gravity. Plainly, his new theory would require some kind of observational verification if it were ever to be accepted.

He thought he knew of one way to do that. In May 1911, Einstein published a paper in the *Annalen* in which he suggested that his theory that gravity would bend rays of light might be tested by photographing the sun during a solar eclipse. Because the sky would be dark enough for the stars to become visible as well, it would be possible to determine whether the visible position of stars appearing close to the sun was different from what their actual position was known to be. The next suitable eclipse would happen over southern Russia in August 1914. But in that same month a more compelling event would intervene—the outbreak of World War I.

The war years would be difficult for Einstein, whose politics were pacifist and internationalist. The jingoism that would infect all levels of German society was apparent just months after the war began, when 93 German intellectuals, including his revered colleague Max Planck, signed a blustery manifesto, "Appeal to the Cultured World," that justified Germany's part in the war. In response, Einstein collaborated with a Jewish physician who was a friend of Löwenthal's to produce a manifesto opposing the war. When it attracted only two other signatories, they abandoned plans to publish it. Einstein consoled himself by joining a fledgling organization, the New Fatherland League, that promoted the idea of a federal union of European nations as a way to discourage future wars. But in 1916 the German government banned the little group because it also advocated a negotiated end to World War I, instead of unconditional German victory.

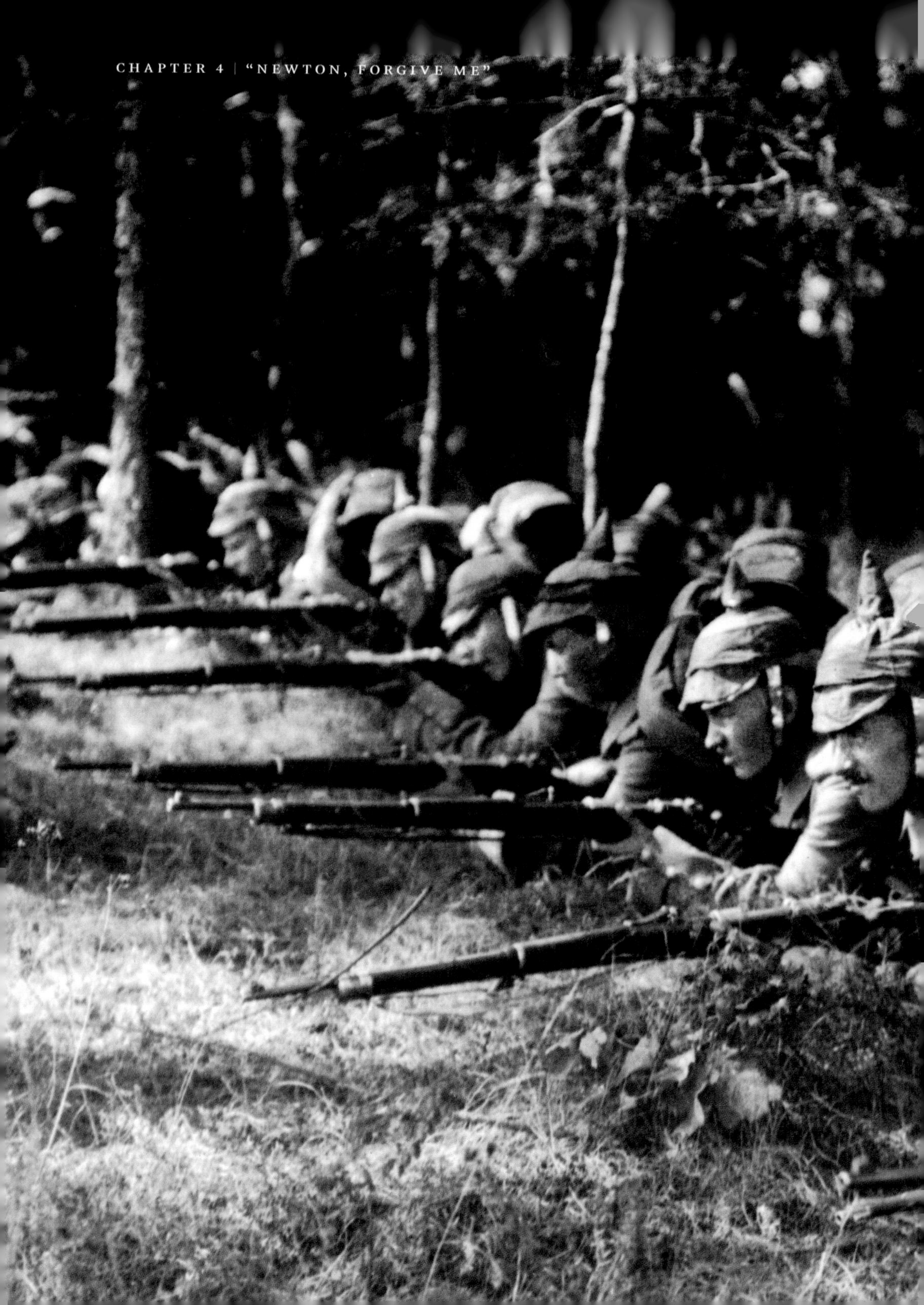

BOGGED DOWN
German soldiers at the front
in 1916. As a pacifist and an
internationalist, Einstein
was strongly opposed to
World War I

IN HIS OWN WORDS

A passage from Einstein's handwritten manuscript of the general theory of relativity

By the following year, Einstein had gone so far as to conclude that an outright German defeat would be preferable to a negotiated peace. He saw that as the only way to discredit the militarism that pervaded German culture. Referring to Prussia's victory over France in the Franco-Prussian War, he wrote to a friend and fellow pacifist, the Nobel Prize–winning French writer Romain Rolland, that Germany "has developed a religion of power through the success of its arms in 1870 and through its successes in trade and industry. This religion dominates nearly all educated people; it has totally replaced the ideals of Goethe's and Schiller's time."

Remarkably, it was amid the depressing tumult of war that Einstein would finalize his general theory of relativity. After publishing the first draft in 1913, he had discovered a number of errors. But by November 1915 he was closing in on solutions. In that month he presented a series of four weekly lectures in Berlin before his fellow members of the Prussian Academy of Sciences. The lectures would detail his efforts to correct those deficiencies—efforts that he was still pursuing during the weeks he was giving the talks. Not until the last of them, on November 25, was he able to present a completely satisfying set of equations to account for the way matter causes space-time to curve and curved space in turn directs the movement of matter. The general theory of relativity, Einstein's greatest intellectual achievement, was now complete.

The following year the general theory would be published by the *Annalen* as a stand-alone volume. Realizing that even many physicists found his new picture of time and space hard to grasp, Einstein also produced a book that attempted to explain it with very little math: *On the Special and the General Theory of Relativity, Generally Comprehensible*. But as he wryly admitted, "generally incomprehensible" might have been a better description. His profound new way of looking at nature, which he described as his "most beautiful discovery," would always remain a challenge to nonspecialists, even the best educated.

By 1917, Einstein was experiencing the first in a series of health problems that would torment him for the next four years and revisit him throughout his life. His various maladies included gallstones, jaundice and stomach problems stemming from an ulcer. After Einstein had dropped nearly 50 pounds, Löwenthal managed to move him into an apartment in her building where she could nurse and feed him. With their lives now even more closely entwined, Einstein began to rethink his promise not to trouble Mileva again about a divorce. He wrote to her in Zurich with an incentive. Feeling certain he would win the Nobel Prize in the next few years, he promised her the entire prize money—135,000 Swedish kronor, a sizable sum—if she would divorce him.

After extensive negotiations through the mail and third parties, in the summer of 1918, Mileva accepted, opening the way at last for Einstein to marry Elsa. They wed the following June, and Einstein moved into the elegant apartment that Elsa shared with her two daughters (where they would always maintain separate bedrooms). Soon they rented two additional attic spaces above their apartment and converted them into a study for Einstein, his "turret room," with book-lined walls and framed prints of his heroes Isaac Newton and Michael Faraday. For the next 17 years, until Elsa's death in 1936, Einstein would be cared for by his nurturing, protective wife, who provided a secure home in which he could work in peace. In return she greatly enjoyed her husband's fame and the social advantages it brought.

But even as Einstein's life became more settled and comfortable, Germany was descending into chaos and hunger, a consequence of its utter defeat in the war, which ended in November 1918. After a brief outburst of revolutionary fury that same month, the Kaiser abdicated, and a republic was declared in the German Reich. At the University of Berlin a worker-student revolutionary council deposed the rector and deans and had them jailed. As a man sympathetic to the socialist aims of the revolutionary movement, but also one whose support for democratic ideals was well known, Einstein put together a three-man contingent of faculty members to go to the Reichstag and plead with the new president of the Reich, Friedrich Ebert, to release their colleagues. An overburdened and distracted Ebert promptly agreed. From there Einstein proceeded to a meeting of the recently revived New Fatherland League. He then delivered a speech warning that the principles of freedom and democracy should not be sacrificed to revolutionary zeal. "All true democrats must stand guard," he said, "lest the old class tyranny of the right be replaced by a new class tyranny of the left."

Meanwhile, with Europe once more at peace, it was possible for Einstein to renew his hope that astronomers somewhere would pursue the observational proof for his theory that a solar eclipse could provide. The abortive attempt of 1914 had been led by a young German astronomer, Erwin Freundlich, who managed to reach Russia only to have his mission thwarted

Going boldly where no man has gone before …

Einstein's general theory of relativity

In 1915, Einstein broadened his special theory of relativity to explain gravity—in a way very different from Newton's concept of a simple force that objects exert on one another.

In 1919 a team led by Cambridge astronomer Arthur Eddington, at left, set out to confirm Einstein's general theory. To do that they photographed a solar eclipse off the coast of West Africa, above. Their pictures proved that starlight was bent by the sun's gravity, just as Einstein had predicted.

Relativity and Gravity

According to relativity theory, gravity is not a force but a warping of space-time, which is an amalgam of time and space. Just as a weight placed on a rubber sheet causes the sheet to bend, any mass stretches the space-time around it. That, in turn, affects the motion of other bodies within that space-time.

Position of star

Observed position of star

1

When starlight passes near a massive body like the sun, the shortest route is a curved line that follows the curvature of space-time. Thus, the starlight appears to an observer on Earth to be coming from a point in the sky different from the star's actual position.

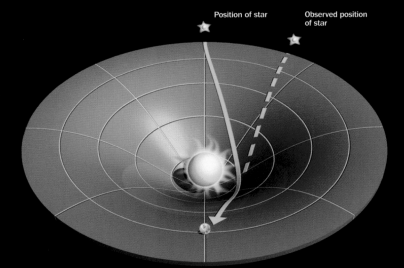

Light entering the black hole

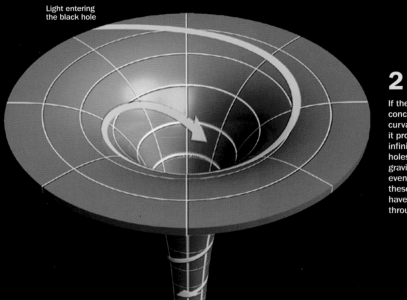

2

If the mass of a star is concentrated enough, the curvature of space-time it produces becomes infinite. Called "black holes" because their gravity is so strong that even light cannot escape, these invisible stars have been discovered throughout the universe.

Graphic by
Joe Lertola and
Arthur Hochstein

STARGAZER
British scientist J.J. Thomson called Einstein's general theory "one of the greatest achievements of human thought."

by the sudden onset of the war. (Freundlich and two German colleagues were actually seized by the Russians as enemy aliens but were exchanged a few weeks later for a group of Russian prisoners of war.) As it turned out, it was a good thing for Einstein that the effort failed, because at the time, he was wrongly calculating that light would be deflected by the sun's gravity by 0.85 second of an arc. The following year he revised his calculations to arrive at the correct number, which was twice that.

As a means to sustain Freundlich's interest in the eclipse project, when Einstein was made head of the newly established Kaiser Wilhelm Institute of Physics late in 1917—the last part of the package of incentives offered by Planck to lure him to Berlin—one of his first acts was to provide the young man a job that would allow him to focus his efforts on relativity's impact on astronomy. But in the end it would be a group of British scientists who made the momentous verification, led by Arthur Stanley Eddington, a Cambridge astronomer who was Einstein's greatest advocate within the English-speaking world. Early in March 1919, Eddington set out from Liverpool with two teams. One headed to the tiny hamlet of Sobral in the Amazon jungle of northwestern Brazil, where a full eclipse would be visible on May 29. Eddington and several other colleagues proceeded to a second observation point, the tiny island of Principe, a Portuguese colony off the coast of West Africa.

At Principe, the eclipse was supposed to begin at 3:13 p.m. local time and last for five minutes. All that morning it rained heavily. As the time for the eclipse neared, however, the sky began clearing—but not entirely. Using a camera with glass-plate negatives, Eddington and his team photographed the eclipse continuously for its full five minutes. All the while, the clouds gathered and parted, revealing and then obscuring the sun and stars. Though the sun was plainly visible in all 16 pictures they took that day, only one was taken at a moment when all the stars were visible as well. But that, in combination with some usable images from Brazil, was enough for Eddington to make measurements that confirmed Einstein's prediction. The stars appeared to be just where he said they would be.

It was not until November 6 that an official announcement of the result was made at a joint meeting in London of the Royal Society, the oldest British scientific institution, and the Royal Astronomical Society. As members of both bodies convened in the great hall at Burlington House, the august headquarters of the Royal Society, a commanding portrait of Sir Isaac Newton gazed down on them. By that date, Einstein and many others within the scientific community were already aware that Eddington's observations had vindicated the general theory, as he always knew they would. But now the news of what J.J. Thomson, the Royal Society's president, would call "one of the greatest achievements of human thought" would be trumpeted to the outside world. The next day the *Times of London* published a front-page story under a triple-decker headline: REVOLUTION IN SCIENCE—NEW THEORY OF THE UNIVERSE—NEWTONIAN IDEAS OVERTHROWN.

With the triumph of the general theory, more than two centuries of scientific certainties were swept away. Proud of his achievement but conscious of his debt to his great predecessor, Einstein would later write: "Newton, forgive me."

Art Meets Science at The Einstein Tower

EFFORTS TO CONFIRM THE
general theory of relativity initially focused
on three applications proposed by Einstein.
The first was that it could explain a small shift
in the orbit of the planet Mercury that had
puzzled scientists since the 1840s. This proof
Einstein accomplished in November 1915.
Then his theory correctly predicted that light
rays would be bent by the sun's gravity, which
was demonstrated by Arthur Eddington's
observation of the solar eclipse in May 1919.
A third potential confirmation involved the
so-called gravitational redshift. According to
Einstein's theory, the frequency of light emitted
by a large body, such as the sun, should decrease
slightly and turn redder as the light struggles
to escape the body's heavy field of gravity. But
to observe that phenomenon would require a
telescope larger than any in Germany at the time.

In order to carry out that final proof, work
began in 1920 on the Einstein Tower, a 46-
foot tower telescope, Europe's first, located
in what is now the Albert Einstein Science
Park in Potsdam. Thoroughly renovated in
1999, it remains a working solar observatory.
It is also a prime example of "Expressionist
architecture," a term describing buildings
from the early decades of the 20th century
that adopted swirling and sometimes
distorted forms—and helped inspire later
work, such as Jørn Utzon's Sydney Opera
House and Frank Gehry's Guggenheim
Museum in Bilbao, Spain.

Einstein, whose artistic tastes were
conservative, never much cared for the white
stucco-clad tower designed by architect Erich
Mendelsohn. And even its state-of-the-art
telescope was not up to the task of detecting
the redshift that Einstein had predicted. It
would be not until 1959, four years after his
death, that scientists at Harvard University,
using laboratory devices, proved him correct
on that score as well.

The Bang Heard 'Round the World

"THIS IS THE WAY the world ends," the poet T.S. Eliot wrote. "Not with a bang but a whimper." Regardless of whether that turns out to be how the world will end, scientists tell us that the universe apparently *began* with a bang—the Big Bang, a picture of how the universe got started that grew out of Einstein's general theory of relativity.

Big Bang thinking first began to take shape in equations published in 1924 by the Russian mathematician Alexander Friedmann. Working with the equations of general relativity, he showed that they did not require a mathematical device that had been introduced into them by Einstein. Called the "cosmological constant," it assumed a kind of antigravity at work in the universe that balances the force of gravity. This allowed Einstein to reconcile his equations with his belief that the universe was static, neither expanding nor contracting, the conclusion supported by astronomical observations at that time. But Friedmann's equations drew a picture of a universe that was constantly changing, either expanding or contracting, depending on whether the total mass density of the universe was very low or very high. Then, in 1927, Georges Lemaitre, a Belgian priest and physicist who was also working out implications of Einstein's theory, decided that the universe must have originated in a sort of "cosmic egg," from which it was still expanding.

The decisive development in Big Bang theory came through the work of the American astronomer Edward Hubble. Through observations he made in the 1920s with the giant telescope at the Mount Wilson Observatory in California, Hubble found that the universe is indeed expanding. All the galaxies we can see are rushing away from our own at speeds that increase with their distance from us. In the face of Hubble's findings, Einstein would disavow his cosmological constant, but in the 1990s physicists realized he was right after all—it correctly describes the presence of "dark energy" that pervades the universe.

So our picture of the first moments of creation now looks like this. About 13.7 billion years ago, the universe emerged from an infinitely small, hot and dense point that astrophysicists call a "singularity." It began its expansion at once, soon producing a mass of subatomic particles like quarks and gluons. Those quickly combined to form protons and neutrons, and within three minutes the first atoms were emerging. Next, the nuclei of hydrogen, the lightest element, began to appear in vast numbers, followed by other light elements. Though all this took just minutes, it was an additional 380,000 years before the hydrogen gas cooled sufficiently to form molecules, and 400 million more before the first stars coalesced.

We are still pursuing ways to enlarge our knowledge of the Big Bang. In 2001, NASA launched the Wilkinson Microwave Anisotropy Probe (WMAP), which provided substantial new information. And scientists hope to learn much more from experiments being performed with the Large Hadron Collider, a massive new particle accelerator that stretches in a 17-mile circuit between Switzerland and France.

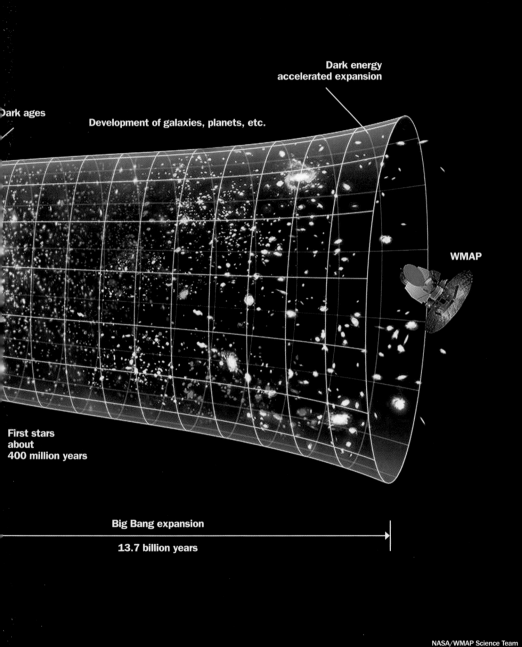

Dark energy
accelerated expansion

Dark ages

Development of galaxies, planets, etc.

WMAP

First stars
about
400 million years

Big Bang expansion

13.7 billion years

NASA/WMAP Science Team

CHAPTER 5

Albert Einstein, Superstar

THE BRITISH ANNOUNCEMENT that Einstein's theories had been vindicated was a watershed not just in Einstein's life but also in the history of the world. He was accustomed by that time to being a prominent figure within the specialized and even somewhat occult field of physics. But now his fame would make an exponential leap into a realm of worldwide celebrity, even among people who had only the foggiest grasp of what relativity was all about. "The world is a curious madhouse," Einstein wrote to his mathematician friend Grossman. "At present every coachman and every waiter argues about whether or not the relativity theory is correct."

MEGAWATTAGE...
Charlie Chaplin, with Einstein and Elsa, at the premiere of City Lights

There were many reasons why the time was right for Einstein. To a Europe weary of war, it seemed a hopeful sign of a rebirth of international cooperation that English scientists had confirmed a theory conceived by a professor at a German university, even if Einstein did hold Swiss citizenship. To the press, Einstein made great copy, somewhat as the Beatles would when they burst on the scene roughly 40 years later. Instead of a dry academic, Einstein turned out to be a kind of beloved uncle, one who happened to be a genius—rumpled, endearing and wryly funny. And to ordinary people, his exotic new picture of reality, however difficult to comprehend, only deepened their sense of wonder when they looked up at the sky. If anything, the difficulties of his theory made Einstein seem more fascinating as a man, something Charlie Chaplin shrewdly explained to him at the Los Angeles premiere of Chaplin's film *City Lights*, which the Einsteins attended as Chaplin's guests in 1931. As the opening night crowds cheered their arrival, Chaplin turned to Einstein, saying, "They cheer me because they all understand me, and they cheer you because nobody understands you."

Soon many prominent scientists and thinkers, including Eddington, Planck and the philosopher Bertrand Russell, were publishing books attempting to explain the theory to ordinary people. Einstein's own popularization from 1916, the one he had impishly called "incomprehensible," was republished in English and became a best seller.

Einstein pretended sometimes to dislike all the attention. He complained to a friend, the physicist Max Born, that "I've been so deluged with questions, invitations, and requests that I dream I'm burning in Hell and the postman is the Devil eternally roaring at me." But as his biographer Walter Isaacson has observed, "Those who truly dislike the public spotlight do not turn up, as the Einsteins eventually would, with Charlie Chaplin on a red carpet."

To Einstein's dismay, relativity also took on a life of its own in a much larger cultural conversation. It became associated in the minds of many people with the spirit behind the social and artistic upheavals of the early 20th century. The Cubism of Picasso, the wild atonal music of Stravinsky and Schoenberg, the fractured literary devices of James Joyce and T.S. Eliot—artists had begun to explode familiar forms of artistic expression in the same way that Einstein had undone the centuries-old assumptions of classical physics. Didn't he give them a kind of scientific validation? Some commentators also began to ask whether Einstein's discovery that space and time were not absolutes but depended on the observer did not in some way vindicate the idea that moral values might be subjective as well, that there could be no way of establishing absolute right and wrong.

Einstein utterly rejected this idea, which he regarded as nothing better than a semantic confusion between relativity and moral relativism. At a London dinner party given in Einstein's honor in 1921, the Archbishop of Canterbury asked the great scientist what implications his theory of relativity had for religion. Einstein was no doubt pleased to have the opportunity to reply: "None. Relativity is a purely scientific matter and has nothing to do with religion."

Not all the attention that Einstein attracted after 1919 was admiring. Amid the upheavals that followed Germany's humiliating defeat in World War I, anti-Jewish feeling was released at all levels of German society. In that toxic atmosphere, even within the scientific community, anti-Semites began to attack relativity theory as "Jewish science" and a hoax. A German ultranationalist named Paul Weyland joined forces with an experimental physicist named Ernst Gehrcke to organize a series of antirelativity meetings around Germany, including a large one in Berlin's Philharmonic Hall, which Einstein attended personally so he could snort at his detractors. Soon one of his most prominent antagonists would be the Nobel Prize–winning physicist

Top: Einstein and Elsa with Hopi Indians in Grand Canyon, Ariz., in March 1931. Clockwise from above left: Einstein with American astronomers at the Mount Wilson Observatory in California, January 1931. Playing the violin, a lifelong passion (sometimes, when invited to speak before an audience, he would instead take out his violin and play something by Mozart or Bach). Receiving an honorary doctorate at Oxford University, May 1931. Sailing, another of his passions, in 1930. After he emigrated to the U.S. in 1933, he had a 17-foot boat called Tinef—Yiddish for piece of junk. Relaxing by the Baltic Sea in 1928.

Philipp Lenard. When he wasn't calling relativity a "Jewish fraud" he was claiming it had actually been discovered by a "pure German" who was killed in the war. In his book *Einstein—A Life*, Denis Brian quotes some of Lenard's typically noxious language: "The Jew conspicuously lacks understanding for the truth, in contrast to the Aryan research scientist with his careful and serious will to truth."

Einstein also found himself the target of unnerving threats. After an anti-Semitic Berliner offered a reward for anyone who succeeded in killing him, a right-wing student at one of Einstein's lectures in Berlin screamed out: "I'm going to cut the throat of that dirty Jew!" Fortunately he didn't follow through.

It didn't help matters that as Einstein's fame grew, he became more willing to speak out on political questions, or that in a Germany bewitched by the mystique of the fatherland and military might, Einstein was a pacifist, an internationalist and a democratic socialist. And though he was not religious in any conventional sense, the escalating persecution of Jews in Europe between the wars, and especially in Germany, made him more aware of himself as a Jew. As he would later write, his relationship to the Jewish people became "my strongest human tie once I achieved complete clarity about our precarious position among the nations."

Increasingly, Einstein also viewed himself as a Zionist, committed to the idea of a Jewish homeland in Palestine. In the Balfour Declaration of 1917, the British government had pledged itself to the establishment of a Jewish homeland there. Four years later, in 1921, Einstein made his first significant contribution to the Zionist cause. At the urging of Chaim Weizmann, president of the London-based World Zionist Organization, he accompanied Weizmann on a tour of the U.S. to raise money for what would become the Hebrew University in Jerusalem.

On April 2, Weizmann and the Einsteins arrived in New York harbor, where they were greeted by the mayor and droves of reporters. Though he spoke no English, through an interpreter he gave an onboard press conference that amused and charmed the press. Next, he was driven in a police motorcade through the streets of the city. There followed nearly two months of travel around the U.S.—with stops in Princeton, N.J.; Boston; Cleveland; and Chicago—and more motorcades, marching bands and flag-draped cars. In Washington he was received at the White House by President Warren G. Harding as part of a delegation from the National Academy of Science. Harding genially admitted to the press that he could not make heads or tails of relativity.

In each city Einstein lectured at local universities and met with the Jewish community, urging people to contribute to the creation of the Hebrew University. Though the trip did not raise as much money as the organizers had hoped—about $750,000 instead of the $4 million goal—it confirmed that Einstein's celebrity extended to North America and gave him a first tantalizing look at the U.S., where—after he was hectored out of Germany by the Nazis—he was destined to spend the final two decades of his life.

In 1922, Einstein had a very unpleasant taste of how difficult life in Germany would become. In June the German Foreign Minister, Walter Rathenau, one of the most prominent Jews in German public life and a close friend of Einstein's, was assassinated by right-wing gunmen. Warned by police that he, too, was on a list of potential targets, Einstein fled Berlin for the relative safety of the coastal city of Kiel. With the anti-Semitic physicist Lenard leading a campaign to bar him from the annual meeting of German scientists, Einstein backed out of a plan to address that gathering.

In part to escape the poisonous atmosphere in Germany, Einstein embarked that fall on a six-month tour of Asia, where he proved to be as much a star as he was in Europe and the U.S.

CONNECTING TO THE TRADITIONS OF HIS PEOPLE
During a 1930 concert at Berlin's Great Synagogue, Einstein wears a Jewish skullcap

In Japan, where the people and culture gave him particular delight, he met with the Emperor and Empress and gave four-hour lectures to adoring throngs. On the way home, he stopped to make the only visit he would ever pay to Palestine. He saw the Wailing Wall in Jerusalem and delivered an address on Mount Scopus that symbolically inaugurated the Hebrew University. But Einstein's future relations with the university would be turbulent, largely because he felt that the school was hiring too many mediocre professors whose main qualification was that they were put forward by wealthy donors.

Starting in 1910, Einstein was nominated repeatedly for the Nobel Prize in Physics. Shortly before his departure for Asia, he learned from a member of the Swedish Academy that in November 1922 he would at last be announced as the winner. Oddly, it would be the prize for 1921, because it had taken the Nobel committee over a year to decide which of Einstein's accomplishments deserved the honor. Relativity was still a touchy matter, still too confounding a theory to the cautious Swedes, who worried that it might be disproved at some future time. In the end they decided that the prize should be awarded instead for Einstein's work on light quanta, the subject of the first of his revolutionary papers of 1905. Despite that, when he gave the Nobel laureate lecture in Sweden in 1923, Einstein pointedly chose relativity as his subject.

One awkward outgrowth of his Nobel Prize was Einstein's discovery that, despite his Swiss citizenship, the German government regarded him as a German citizen as well, largely because in 1920 he had sworn an oath on both the German and the Prussian constitutions. Another complication was that Mileva and the boys were unhappy that Einstein, while keeping his promise to transfer the prize money entirely to his ex-wife, had done so through a trust fund that allowed her to withdraw only the interest. In the end, the money went to buy three multifamily homes in Zurich. The rents would ensure Mileva and their sons a comfortable living, at least for a number of years. After World War II, in the last years of her life, money would become a problem again.

Meanwhile, the political situation in Germany was becoming increasingly sinister. In November 1923, Einstein was in the Dutch city of Leiden, where he spent several months each year as a visiting professor. That same month, in Munich, Adolf Hitler and his Brownshirts made the abortive coup attempt known as the Beer Hall Putsch. Days later Hitler was arrested and charged with treason. He would spend nine months in prison, time he would devote to working on his toxic personal testament *Mein Kampf.* His initial attempt to take power in Germany may have ended in failure, but the world had not heard the last of him.

In one important area of Einstein's continuing work in theoretical physics, the 1920s would prove to be a period of mostly fruitless endeavor. By the middle of that decade he was increasingly absorbed in an effort to reconcile his new theory of gravity with Maxwell's theory of electromagnetism—to produce what's called a unified field theory. This would mean finding a common thread in the laws that governed the very largest bodies, like stars and planets, and those that applied to the infinitesimal world of atoms. It was an undertaking that would consume him for many years—and would come to nothing in his lifetime.

And while he struggled down this path, another scientific revolution was bursting out around him, quantum mechanics, one that would soon triumph—and make him profoundly uncomfortable, even though it had been set in motion by his own early work on light quanta. The main lines of quantum mechanics were first sketched out in 1925 by a young German physicist, Werner Heisenberg. Two years later Heisenberg would produce his famous "uncertainty principle," which asserts that we cannot know the precise position of a particle and its velocity in the same instant. More, the very act of observing a particle like an electron affects it, because the photons of the light required to see the electron knock it out of the atom.

In 1905, when Einstein published his light quanta paper, it was he who was at the forefront of quantum theory. But as he grew older, the dauntless thinker who had once challenged Newton became more reluctant to overturn the centuries-old assumptions of physics. This was the very thing quantum mechanics was doing, putting in their place a universe that operated in bizarre ways he could not abide. In quantum theory, particles can exchange information and coordinate their properties instantly, no matter how far apart they are. To Einstein this smacked of Newton's discredited idea of forces that propagate instantly through space, or as he would call it "spooky action at a distance." And if Heisenberg's uncertainty principle was correct, there was no objective reality at all, merely our imperfect observations. The Danish physicist Niels Bohr, whose "Copenhagen interpretation" of quantum physics would become widely influential, even proposed that, until it is observed, a quantum system exists merely as a set of probabilities. Only at the moment of observation does it snap into existence. Einstein found this absurd. Does the moon not exist, he asked, until a mouse sees it?

Worse, quantum mechanics proposed a universe that was essentially random, one in which an electron can jump out of its orbit at any time or appear to be in two locations in the same instant. All this offended Einstein's sense of order and causality in nature, the idea of predictability dating back to Newton. He told the wife of his physicist friend Max Born that

QUANTUM QUANDARIES
Einstein, above, in his Berlin study, could not bring himself to accept the "uncertainty principle" of Werner Heisenberg, right

he could not accept her husband's idea "that an electron exposed to radiation should choose of its own free will not only its moment to jump off, but also its direction." If that were so, he said, he would rather be a cobbler or work in a gambling casino. In 1927 and again in 1930, the Solvay Conference of European physicists turned into a days-long debate between Einstein and the Danish physicist Bohr. Unnerved by the role of chance in quantum physics, Einstein announced a sentiment he would repeat many times, "God does not play dice with the world." Bohr shot back, "Stop telling God what to do."

Yet Einstein's pioneering work continued to spur advances in physics by younger men—including, ironically, advances in quantum mechanics. Inspired by Einstein's discovery that light could have the quality of both a wave and a particle, the young French physicist Louis de Broglie determined that matter did as well. Particles like electrons, photons or protons could all be regarded as waves. Einstein embraced the idea of De Broglie's "matter waves." Soon the Austrian physicist Erwin Schrödinger developed equations to describe them, for the first time giving scientists a means to draw a detailed picture of the interior of an atom. Einstein continued to make important contributions of his own as well. By extending an idea first introduced

ON THE PROWL
Hitler, with his henchmen Ernst Röhm and Heinrich Himmler, in 1930

ON THE ROAD
As they depart for New York
in 1931, the Einsteins get a
send-off at Pasadena Station

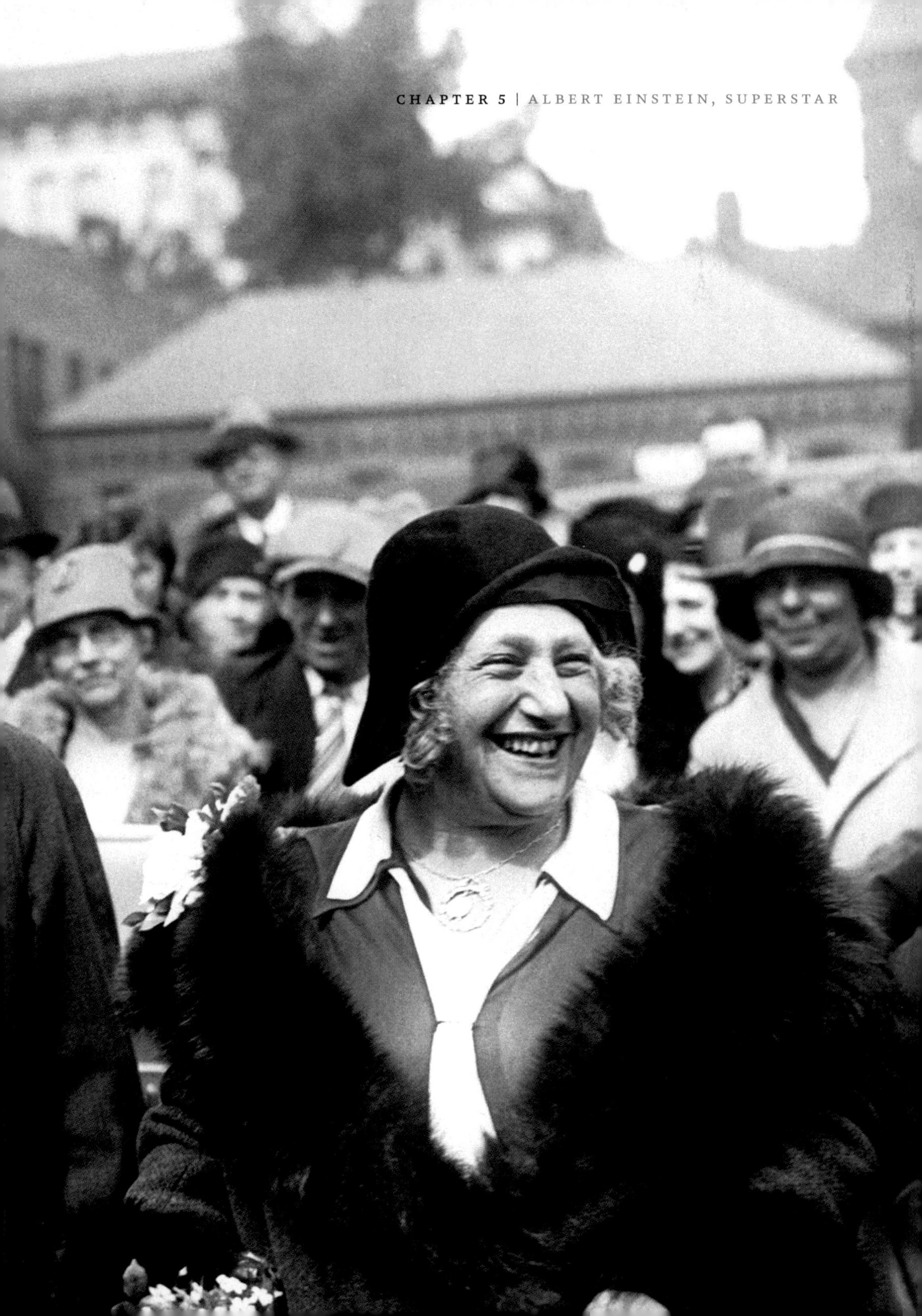

to him in the mid-1920s by a young Indian physicist, Satyendra Nath Bose, he predicted that at ultra-low temperatures, atoms in a dilute gas would decline to the lowest energy state and form a single "super-atom"—a prediction, the Bose-Einstein condensation, that was finally confirmed in 1995.

His increasingly isolated position within the scientific community was not the only source of difficulty for Einstein in those years. During a trip to Switzerland in April 1928, he collapsed while lugging his heavy suitcase up a steep hill. Though the problem would turn out not to be a heart attack, it was a sign of cardiac trouble. His doctor assigned him to prolonged bed rest back home in Berlin. Before long, his wife Elsa, exhausted from nursing him, hired 32-year-old Helen Dukas, the sister of a friend, to assist her. Dukas would become virtually one of the family. She remained with Einstein as his devoted aide until his death in 1955, taking care of all his workaday needs—correspondence, errands, interview requests—so that he could devote himself fully to his work. After his death, as one of the executors of estate, she would dedicate herself to preserving what some biographers considered to be a sanitized version of his memory.

His four-month convalescence gave Einstein an opportunity to focus again on his attempt to develop a unified field theory. By January of 1929 he was ready to submit a paper to the Prussian Academy with what he believed might be a solution. He optimistically told an English newspaper that his new work proved at last that "the force which moves electrons in their ellipses about the nuclei of atoms is the same force which moves our earth in its annual course about the sun, and is the same force which brings to us the light and heat which makes life possible upon this planet."

The prospect that Einstein might once again have solved a major scientific riddle galvanized the press and public all around the world. When the academy published his paper at the end of the month, all six pages were posted in the window of a London department store so that crowds on the street could try to decipher it. But Einstein's colleagues in the scientific community were not impressed. For one thing, in order to arrive at his new theory, Einstein had violated rules established by his own general theory of relativity. Within a few years even he was obliged to admit that he had failed once more.

In 1929, Einstein turned 50. He was able to celebrate with the acquisition that summer of a small plot of land in the village of Caputh, south of Potsdam. There he would build a country house and dock the much appreciated sailboat that was a birthday gift from a group of friends. Though Einstein was willing to hire an architect working in a modern style, he refused the furniture produced by the famous Bauhaus designer Marcel Breuer, complaining that it reminded him of a "machine shop or a hospital operating room." His modern house would be furnished with old-fashioned castoffs from his Berlin apartment.

By now there were strains in Einstein's marriage to Elsa, caused in large part by his constant dalliances with other women. For a time around 1924, he fell powerfully in love with his new secretary, Betty Neumann. Soon after, he began a relationship that went on for years with Toni Mendel, a wealthy widow close to his own age. Then there was Ethel Michanowski, a Berlin socialite who pursued him aggressively, and an Austrian, Margarete Lebach, whose arrivals in Caputh would prompt Elsa to decamp for shopping trips in Berlin. Elsa tolerated these affairs because in most other respects their life together was a good one, though also, as she once said, "exhausting and complicated, and not only in one way but in others."

Einstein's misgivings about marriage in general may have contributed to his opposition to the decision by his son Hans Albert to marry Frieda Knecht, a curt, unattractive woman nine years his senior. Einstein bluntly predicted to his son that he would one day decide to leave his prospective bride. He even implored him not to have children with her. He may have been recalling his own parents' opposition to his marriage to Mileva, which eventually turned out to be well justified. All the same, Hans Albert and Frieda married in 1927, had children and stayed together until her death in 1958. And despite his initial misgivings, Einstein came to accept her.

Relations with his younger son had become troubled by this time as well. Eduard was living at home with his mother while studying medicine at Zurich University in hope of becoming a psychiatrist. But he was becoming increasingly depressed and withdrawn, even threatening once to jump out his bedroom window. Einstein was greatly distressed by his son's deterioration but felt helpless.

Meanwhile, the political situation in Germany was also taking a turn for the worse. Runaway inflation had long since ceased to be a problem, but by 1930 the worldwide Depression was making its effects felt, leading to high unemployment. In elections in September, Hitler's National Socialist Party, once an insignificant splinter group, won 6 million votes, 18% of the total.

By December, Einstein and Elsa were traveling again, making their second trip to the U.S., this time at the invitation of the California Institute of Technology, in Pasadena, Calif. Einstein had agreed to spend two months there as a well-paid research associate. His stopover in New York was once again tumultuous, marked by celebrations and speeches, including a controversial address about pacifism in which he urged others to refuse compulsory military service. "Even if only 2% of those assigned to perform military service should announce their refusal to fight," he said, "governments would be powerless. They would not dare send such a large number of people to jail." His speech became a rallying cry for war resisters, spurring young men to start wearing "2%" buttons on their lapels.

Einstein was delighted by California. He was greeted in San Diego with a four-hour welcoming ceremony, complete with flower-decked floats and waving mermaids. Hollywood offered him movie roles. (All were declined.) He frequently visited the Mount Wilson Observatory, perched high on the edge of the Sierra Nevadas, where the astronomer Edwin Hubble had been making phenomenal observations of the heavens with his 100-inch reflecting telescope. (When the astronomers there boasted that their telescope could probe the structure of the universe, Elsa quipped: "My husband does that on the back of an old envelope.") But he strained his relations with Caltech's politically conservative president, Robert A. Millikan, whose school depended heavily on donations from wealthy conservatives. Already unhappy about the 2% speech in New York, Millikan was equally displeased when Einstein befriended the left-wing American novelist Upton Sinclair and agreed to be interviewed by him for a socialist weekly.

The Germany that Einstein returned to in the spring of 1931 was continuing its downward spiral. Parliament had been dissolved; Nazis and leftists were brawling in the streets. For the next two years Einstein continued to advocate for pacifist positions and to cooperate fitfully with leftist groups. He also made one of the greatest blunders of his public life: having signed an appeal in 1930 that denounced Stalin's monstrous show trials of fellow Bolsheviks, Einstein was somehow persuaded a year later to recant his criticism of the trials.

By the end of 1931 Einstein was again en route to America for another two-month stint at Caltech. By that time he was thinking of leaving Germany for good. He had offers of permanent positions from Caltech and Oxford. Soon there would be another, very intriguing one. In California he was visited by Abraham Flexner, a man who had enjoyed significant influence over American higher education as head of a Rockefeller Foundation board that gave sizable gifts to universities. Now he was about to use a $5 million donation from the department-store heirs Louis Bamberger and his sister Caroline to establish a new institute, a "haven" where scholars could pursue their researches without the distraction of teaching duties. The Institute for Advanced Study was to be located in Princeton, N.J., with the agreement of Princeton University but independent of it. There was no discussion yet of a position there for Einstein, but the possibility hung in the air.

Einstein and Flexner agreed to meet again in Oxford the following spring to talk further about the institute. During that conversation, Flexner at last popped the question: Would Einstein entertain the possibility of joining? One month later Flexner turned up in Caputh to finalize the offer. In the end, it was agreed that Einstein would spend six months each year at the institute, at a salary of $10,000. (Louis Bamberger would later insist on increasing the sum to $15,000.) At Einstein's urging, the institute would also provide a position for Walther Mayer, a young mathematician from Vienna who had become his assistant and, as Einstein liked to refer to him, "the calculator."

The offer from the institute came none too soon. In elections that July the Nazis won 37% of the vote and became the largest party in the Reichstag. But even as they edged ever closer to power, Einstein struggled to sustain his pacifist ideals. In a published exchange of letters with his friend Sigmund Freud, he again put forward his belief that to avoid future wars, nations must surrender some of their sovereignty to an international organization that had genuine power to enforce its decisions.

There was briefly an unforeseen obstacle to Einstein's departure from Germany. When news of his appointment to the institute became public in the U.S., right-wing groups objected to allowing this well-known pacifist and socialist to enter the country. A certain Mrs. Randolph Frothingham, head of the Woman Patriot Corporation, sent a 16-page memo to the U.S. State Department detailing Einstein's association with leftist organizations. Her complaint was forwarded to the American consulate in Berlin, which indeed refused to issue a visa to Einstein until he agreed to sign a declaration swearing that he was not a member of any radical organization.

Visa in hand, Einstein made preparations to depart with Elsa for America in December. Despite the accelerating threat of the Nazis, he was still telling friends that they were not leaving Germany for good and that he expected to return to Berlin in April. But in his heart he suspected otherwise. As he and Elsa were closing up their house in Caputh for the winter, he turned to her. "Take a very good look at it," he said. "You will never see it again."

FACING THE UNKNOWN
Einstein on the beach in Santa Barbara, Calif., in 1933, the year he fled Germany

CHAPTER 6

"I've Done My Share"

O N JANUARY 30, 1933, SHORTLY after Einstein and Elsa arrived again in Pasadena, Adolf Hitler was made the new Chancellor of Germany. Less than a month later, the Reichstag was in flames. The Nazis claimed that leftists had set the fire, providing a pretext for Hitler to suspend civil liberties in Germany and over time establish his dictatorship. Europe's fate was sealed. Though he wasn't yet entirely ready to accept it, so was Einstein's.

On March 10, in remarks reported worldwide, Einstein spoke to a journalist in California. "As long as I have any choice in the matter," he said, "I shall live only in a country where civil

THE LION IN WINTER
Einstein in Princeton in 1948,
in a portrait by LIFE magazine
photographer Alfred Eisenstadt

THE ROAD FROM EUROPE ...
From left: Einstein in 1933 with his British host, Oliver Locker-Lampson, who provided armed guards to ensure Einstein's safety; Einstein's close friend Queen Elisabeth of Belgium

liberty, tolerance and equality of all citizens before the law prevail. These conditions do not exist in Germany at the present time." One day later, with his second stay at Caltech completed, he and his wife were on a train headed for New York City, where they would board a ship bound for Antwerp, Belgium. But despite his widely reported words, he still planned to make his way ultimately to Berlin. En route cross-country he and Elsa learned that Nazi storm troopers had ransacked their Berlin apartment. In New York the German consul warned Einstein: "If you go to Germany, Albert, they'll drag you through the streets by the hair."

Even so, he and his wife boarded ship for home. Did Einstein still somehow hope that Hitler might retract his claws? By that time even Elsa's daughters had fled Germany. While they were crossing the Atlantic, the Einsteins got word that their house in Caputh had also been raided by the Nazis on the improbable suspicion that it was being used to store weapons for the communists. Incriminating evidence was produced—a bread knife. Next Einstein's sailboat was seized on the grounds that it could be used for smuggling. Now at last he was certain. He could not return.

Arriving in Belgium in late March, Einstein headed for Brussels and the German consulate, where he declared he was renouncing the German citizenship that he thought he had shed once and for all as a teenager. Then he sent a letter to the Prussian Academy announcing his resignation. In Germany, meanwhile, things were going from bad to worse. A new law forbade Jews from holding official positions, including professorships like the one Einstein had in Berlin. In May the book burnings began. Einstein's works, naturally, were among the titles tossed into the flames. Then Einstein's chief antagonist, the anti-Semitic physicist Philipp Lenard, was chosen by Hitler to be Germany's new head of Aryan science.

While he considered his options—which, in addition to his new position in Princeton, included offers from universities in Britain, Holland and Spain—Einstein and Elsa lived for several months in a rented seaside house in Le Coq sur Mer, near Ostend, where they were joined by Elsa's daughters. He used the time to resume a close friendship with King Albert and Queen Elisabeth of Belgium, whom he had met and warmed to on earlier visits. He and

... TO AMERICA
Speaking at London's Royal Albert Hall in October 1933, just before departing Europe for the last time; arriving in New York a few weeks later; the Einstein home in Princeton, N.J.

the music-loving queen enjoyed playing Mozart together, and Einstein was delighted by the relative simplicity of the royal household. In light of the continual threats being made against Einstein in Germany, the royal couple arranged for police protection for him in Le Coq sur Mer.

While Einstein was still in Belgium, a controversy over a pair of Belgian conscientious objectors gave him an opportunity to make public a significant change in his position on pacifism. Urged by antiwar groups to speak on behalf of the imprisoned men, he issued a letter declaring that "the present threatening situation, created by the events in Germany," meant that armed forces like Belgium's were "urgently needed." His widely reported about-face shocked pacifists all across Europe and North America.

That spring Einstein made a trip to Zurich to see his son Eduard, who was in a mental hospital with a diagnosis of schizophrenia. Einstein was convinced that his son's problems were an inheritance from his mother and that little could be done to help him. In a letter to his friend Michele Besso, he wrote that he had seen his son's illness "coming slowly but inexorably" since Eduard was a boy. His visit to Zurich would be the last time he would ever see him or his former wife Mileva.

In 1933, Einstein made three trips to England, the first to deliver several lectures, the second at the invitation of Oliver Locker-Lampson, a member of Parliament and an avid anti-Nazi who brought Einstein to lunch with Winston Churchill at Churchill's home. Not surprisingly, Einstein and Churchill saw eye-to-eye on the menace represented by Hitler. "He is an eminently wise man," Einstein wrote to Elsa. "It became clear to me that these people have made preparations and are determined to act resolutely and soon." Einstein returned to England in September to spend a month at Locker-Lampson's vacation home on the Norfolk coast before setting sail once more for the U.S. with Elsa. At the time, he still intended to come back to Europe the following spring. But, in fact, he would never return.

No sooner had Einstein arrived in New York harbor than he got a first taste of what would become an increasing source of tension between himself and Abraham Flexner, director of the Institute for Advanced Studies. The problems would grow out of Flexner's aggressive attempts to prevent Einstein from making potentially embarrassing public statements on issues of the day. Though a welcoming party was waiting for his ship when it docked—complete with the mayor of New York, who planned to lead a parade—Flexner arranged for Einstein to be spirited away via tugboat to a car waiting at the southern tip of Manhattan. Even before the ship arrived, he had cabled Einstein: "Make no statement and give no interviews on any subject."

Flexner's sensitivity on the matter grew out of his conviction that if Einstein appeared to be seeking publicity, it could provoke anti-Semitism in the U.S. Flexner was Jewish himself but thoroughly assimilated and very careful not to give offense to non-Jews. He went so far as to intercept Einstein's mail so he could turn down invitations to public gatherings on Einstein's behalf—and without his knowledge. The last straw was his attempt to prevent Einstein from accepting an invitation to meet with President Franklin Roosevelt at the White House. When Flexner learned of the offer—again by opening Einstein's mail—he not only took it upon himself to call Roosevelt's social secretary and decline on Einstein's behalf but also wrote a letter to FDR insisting that Einstein must not be disturbed.

When Einstein learned what had happened, he was furious. He contacted Eleanor Roosevelt directly to communicate his willingness to visit the President. She extended another invitation, and the Einsteins arrived at the White House on January 24, 1934, for dinner with the Roosevelts and an overnight stay. Before making the trip to Washington, Einstein sent a letter to the trustees of the institute threatening to quit if Flexner's interference in his affairs did not cease. That put an end to Flexner's meddling, but it also soured their relations for good.

ADMIRED ANTAGONIST
Einstein respected Niels Bohr but sparred with him over quantum physics

His difficulties with Flexner aside, Einstein found the institute to be a very congenial place. He liked being able to pursue pure research without teaching duties. And with its handsome homes and the Gothic Revival spires of its campus, the town of Princeton appealed to him as well, even if he found himself amused by the local society. "A quaint and ceremonious village of puny demigods," he called it in one letter, "strutting on stiff legs." By the spring of 1934 he had decided to settle in permanently at the institute and become a full professor, instead of a visitor who stayed just five months each year.

Einstein would remain in Princeton for the rest of his life. Summers he spent happily in various rented houses on the shores of Rhode Island, Connecticut or Long Island, places where he could indulge his love of sailing. He would never see Europe again, though in 1934, Elsa traveled to Paris to be at the deathbed of her daughter Ilse, who was succumbing to leukemia. (On her return Elsa would bring with her boxes of Einstein's personal papers that her daughter Margot and members of the anti-Nazi underground had smuggled out of Germany.) Soon Margot also came to the U.S.

Although they had rented a place to live during their first years in Princeton, the Einsteins now purchased a modest white clapboard house at 112 Mercer Street, where the great man had a second-floor study with a picture-window view across wooded parkland. In these years Einstein fully entered into his later-life role as a beloved local eccentric, Princeton's own absent-minded professor. With his unmistakable shock of unkempt hair, he could be seen on any day walking about town—he didn't drive—often without socks, lost in thought. Sometimes literally lost: an embarrassed Einstein is said to have called the institute one day to get directions back to his own house.

Scarcely had the Einsteins moved into their new home than Elsa had serious heart and kidney problems diagnosed that worsened steadily. Einstein was distraught. "He wanders around like a lost soul," Elsa wrote to a friend. "I never thought he loved me so much. And that comforts me." In Elsa's final weeks Einstein sat by her bedside talking and reading to her. On the evening of December 20, 1936, during a heavy snowstorm, she slipped away.

After Elsa's death, Einstein's household consisted of Helen Dukas and Elsa's daughter Margot. In 1938 they were joined by his sister Maja, who had been living in Florence until Mussolini withdrew resident status from all foreign Jews. That same year Einstein's son Hans Albert, his wife Frieda and their two young boys also came to the U.S., where Hans Albert would find work studying soil conservation for the U.S. Department of Agriculture in Clemson, S.C. Not long after their arrival, they suffered a grievous blow. At his wife's urging, Hans Albert had become a Christian Scientist. When their six-year-old son Klaus contracted diphtheria, they refused medical care for him, and he died. But the tragedy helped bring Einstein closer to Hans Albert, who would go on to become a professor of engineering at Caltech and then at Berkeley.

The year after Elsa's death, Einstein had a distinguished overnight visitor. In Princeton to perform a concert, the singer Marian Anderson was refused a room at the Nassau Inn, the best hotel in town, because she was black. Einstein, whose time in America had made him increasingly aware of the nation's racial problems, invited her to stay at his house. Two years later Anderson would make civil rights history. Barred by the Daughters of the American Revolution from performing before an integrated audience at Constitution Hall in Washington, she accepted Franklin and Eleanor Roosevelt's invitation to give a free outdoor concert on the steps of the Lincoln Memorial before 75,000 people and millions more on radio. In years to come, whenever Anderson was in Princeton, she stayed at Einstein's home.

From his perch at Princeton in the 1930s, Einstein continued to resist the ever growing authority of quantum mechanics among physicists. In yet another effort to cast doubt on the quantum explanation of nature, in 1935 he published a paper containing what has come to be known as the Einstein-Podolsky-Rosen Paradox, because it was written with two colleagues from the institute, Boris Podolsky, a physicist, and Nathan Rosen, a young mathematician. Einstein was deeply troubled by a central belief of Niels Bohr, the Danish physicist whose "Copenhagen interpretation" of quantum mechanics was gaining ever wider assent within the field. Bohr held that until they were observed, particles existed merely as probabilities, a blend of all possible states. Only at the moment of observation did they assume their final state.

But, Einstein asked, what if it were possible to learn something about a particle—for instance, its position—without observing it? Wouldn't that position be a physical reality, not a mere probability? He suggested the example of two particles that have been emitted in opposite directions from a decaying atom that is at rest. If at a particular moment you determined the speed of the first particle, you would know the speed of the second, because you would know it's been moving at the same speed. And if you measured the position of the second , you would know both the position and the velocity of the first: something quantum theory says is impossible. And under quantum theory, observing one particle can somehow instantly affect a second particle across vast distances. But under relativity theory, no signal can travel faster than the speed of light.

Bohr's eventual reply made quantum mechanics seem even more bizarre—everything in the universe, even particles separated by many millions of miles, was "entangled." Einstein would never accept this. He continued to promote his contrary view of reality in *The Evolution of Physics,* a very successful history textbook that he wrote in 1938 with Leopold Infeld, a Jewish refugee from Poland who had suggested the project.

By the summer of 1939, despite all efforts to appease Hitler, Europe was on the brink of war once again. In July two physicist friends came to visit Einstein at the vacation home he was renting that year on the eastern tip of Long Island. Eugene Wigner and Leo Szilard were both Hungarian refugees. Szilard had been working at Columbia University on the possibility of producing a nuclear chain reaction that could unleash the immense power of the atom. Both men knew that the year before, German scientists had discovered it was possible to produce a fission reaction using uranium.

Fearing that the Germans would now pursue work on an atomic bomb, and knowing that the Belgian Congo was a major source of uranium, Szilard hoped Belgium could be persuaded to bar the export of uranium to Germany. He and Wigner had traveled to Long Island to enlist Einstein to contact his old friend Queen Elisabeth of Belgium. (She was now the queen mother—her husband had died in 1934 and been succeeded by their son Leopold.) Einstein suggested instead that they send a letter to the Belgian government by way of the U.S. State Department. But before they could follow through, Szilard met in Washington with Alexander Sachs, an economist who was a friend of Roosevelt's. Sachs suggested they should be writing directly to the President and offered to hand-deliver a letter if they did.

Szilard returned to Einstein's house on Long Island, this time in the company of another Hungarian refugee physicist, Edward Teller. Einstein dictated a letter in German that Teller took down. Szilard later translated it into English and sent Einstein two versions, one of them 45 lines long, the other 25. Einstein signed both.

It would not be until October 11 that Sachs would manage to meet with the President. By that time Germany had invaded Poland, and Europe was at war. To make sure he had Roosevelt's attention, at their meeting, Sachs read Einstein's words—in the longer version—out loud. The letter informed the President that scientists could very soon produce a nuclear chain reaction and that "extremely powerful bombs of a new type may thus be constructed." Before closing, Einstein suggested that Roosevelt might want to establish regular contact "between the administration and the group of physicists working on chain reactions in America." Roosevelt immediately called in his assistant, General Edwin Watson, and told him: "This requires action."

As a first step, Roosevelt established a board with representatives of the Army and Navy as well as Szilard, Teller and Wigner, plus the University of Chicago physicist Enrico Fermi, a refugee from Mussolini's Fascism. Einstein was not included, and when he was invited to join the following year, he declined. Though his letter to FDR was important in spurring the American effort to build an atomic weapon, Einstein played no direct role

YOUR ATTENTION, PLEASE
The first page of Einstein's letter to FDR about the possibility of atomic weapons

THE FATHER OF THE BOMB—AND THE GODFATHER
*After heading weapons research for the Manhattan Project, J. Robert Oppenheimer, here with
Einstein in 1947, became director of the Institute for Advanced Studies*

in what would eventually become the Manhattan Project.

One reason Einstein was excluded from the A-bomb effort, which did not get seriously
under way until just before the U.S. entered the war in 1941, was that he was considered a security risk. In the summer of 1940, General Sherman Miles, who was organizing the committee
of nuclear scientists ordered up by Roosevelt, asked FBI Director J. Edgar Hoover what was in
Einstein's FBI file. Hoover provided Miles with the accusatory letter drawn up years earlier by
the Woman Patriot Corporation. He also wrongly claimed that Einstein had been at the 1932
World Antiwar Congress in Amsterdam—a meeting Einstein had vehemently and publicly declined to attend because he felt it was intended to glorify the Soviet Union. All the same, Hoover
labeled Einstein an "extreme radical."

Ironically, not long after, on October 1, Einstein was sworn in as a U.S. citizen, along with
Elsa's daughter Margot and Helen Dukas. As physicists all around the country disappeared into
the top secret Manhattan Project, Einstein would find other ways to contribute to the war effort. In 1943 he became a $25-a-day consultant to the U.S. Navy's Bureau of Ordnance, a job that
did not require a security clearance. Tasked to evaluate proposed weaponry, he worked on ideas
for detonating torpedoes more effectively. To help raise money for war bonds, he also agreed to
handwrite a new copy of his 1905 paper on the special theory of relativity. (In keeping with his

AT HIS LEISURE
Einstein in his study at Princeton in 1951. On the wall behind him is a picture of fellow pacifist Mahatma Gandhi, whom he greatly admired

practice as a young man, he had discarded the original manuscript soon after it was published.) At auction, the copy was bought for a phenomenal $6.5 million by an insurance company that donated it to the Library of Congress.

As the war progressed, Einstein's feelings toward Germany became increasingly bitter. "The Germans as a whole nation are responsible for these mass murders," he wrote, "and must be punished for them as a nation, if there is any justice in the world." (After the war, though he remained on close terms with individual Germans, he refused all invitations to join German scientific organizations. He even forbade publication of his books in Germany.) Fortunately, the German effort to produce an atomic weapon was called off, while the U.S. tested a successful version in July 1945. In August the bombs were dropped on Hiroshima and then Nagasaki, leading to the surrender of Japan.

When Einstein heard the news about Hiroshima, his only reply was "Oh, *weh*" (oh, my God). Though he had played a role in bringing it about, he would be deeply uncomfortable with the way postwar America associated him with the fearsome new weapon. Both TIME and *Newsweek* put him on their covers in ways that presented him as a sort of godfather of the bomb. Determined not to seem an accomplice to Armageddon, Einstein became even more outspoken on the need for a global authority of some kind as the way to prevent nuclear war. "The only salvation for civilization," he told a reporter, "lies in the creation of world government." He began to develop detailed ideas about how that might be done. The U.S., Britain and the Soviet Union should form the government, he proposed, then invite other nations to join. At the request of Leo Szilard, he became chairman of a new organization, the Emergency Committee of Atomic Scientists, dedicated to nuclear arms control. But by the end of 1948, after issuing many appeals and proclamations, the group suspended its activities.

By that time Einstein was in his twilight years. In the spring of 1946 he was retired by the institute, though with full salary and use of all facilities there. By the fall its new director would be J. Robert Oppenheimer, who had headed the weapons laboratory of the Manhattan Project. Oppenheimer was a man Einstein liked and admired, but the young physicists he attracted to the institute were by now all devoted to quantum mechanics. To them, Einstein, with his continued refusal to accept the new science, was a revered but antiquated figure, a great man gathering dust. Or as Oppenheimer put it: "a landmark but not a beacon."

Then Einstein's health began to deteriorate. A prolonged bout of stomach complaints led him to undergo surgery in 1948 that revealed a sizable aneurysm, a grapefruit-size swelling of the major intestinal aorta. Though his doctors supposed rightly that it would eventually prove fatal, its size and location made surgery too dangerous a treatment option. That same year Einstein's first wife Mileva died of a stroke in Zurich. Their son Eduard would languish in a psychiatric hospital there until his death in 1965. Einstein's sister Maja, who continued to live with him in Princeton, suffered a stroke that kept her bedridden until her death in 1951.

The year 1950 marked the beginning of the Red Scare in the U.S., after the Soviet Union had successfully tested an atomic weapon and Senator Joseph McCarthy had set off the seemingly endless witch hunt for clandestine communists. Shortly after President Harry Truman committed the U.S. to developing a hydrogen bomb, Einstein appeared on a new television show hosted by Eleanor Roosevelt to warn that the arms race could result in "general annihilation" and to complain about a growing repression of opinion across America.

As Einstein's pronouncements often did, his statements made headlines around the world, which attracted the attention once more of Hoover. Though Einstein was unaware of the

SUFFER THE LITTLE CHILDREN TO COME UNTO ME
On his 70th birthday, Einstein is visited by a group of young Holocaust refugees

fact, the year before, Hoover had failed to establish that Einstein was a communist sympathizer and then launched a probe into Einstein's secretary, Helen Dukas, looking in vain for evidence that she was a Soviet spy. Now Hoover ordered a renewed investigation into Einstein and his possible connections to communists—a suspicion that ignored his frequent and forceful denunciations of the Soviet Union and his refusal to visit there. In the end the FBI file on Einstein would grow to 1,427 pages, none of them containing anything of consequence.

As Einstein biographer Walter Isaacson points out, however, Hoover had failed to discover that Einstein did have one unwitting connection to an actual Soviet spy. Margarita Konenkova was a Russian living in New York and assigned by Moscow to influence American scientists. Introduced to Einstein by his stepdaughter Margot, she embarked in 1941 on a lengthy affair with him that continued until she returned to the Soviet Union in 1945. But no evidence has emerged that Einstein passed on any information to Konenkova, deliberately or unknowingly, and in any event, he was unconnected to the Manhattan Project that might well have interested her.

In 1952, Einstein was proffered an honor he could not accept. Despite his early involvement with Zionism, by the late 1930s he was expressing misgivings in public about a Jewish state "with borders, an army, and a measure of temporal power." But once the state of Israel was established in 1948, Einstein came around. Upon the death of Israel's first President, Chaim Weizmann, Israeli Prime Minister David Ben-Gurion decided to offer Einstein the presidency, a largely ceremonial office. But Einstein sent a letter of regret, protesting that "I lack both the natural aptitude and the experience to deal properly with people and to exercise official functions."

By that time he also lacked the energy for a life of public appearances. But in his final years Einstein would occasionally devote himself to speaking on behalf of people he saw as victims of the anticommunist hysteria sweeping America. When Julius and Ethel Rosenberg were convicted of giving atomic secrets to the Russians, he wrote privately to the judge in their trial, asking him to spare them the death penalty. When they were sentenced to die, he wrote to outgoing President Truman, asking for clemency. But when that letter went public, it prompted an avalanche of angry letters addressed to Einstein. The Rosenbergs would be executed during the presidency of Truman's successor, Dwight Eisenhower.

Another letter from Einstein went to William Frauenglass, a Brooklyn schoolteacher who had refused to answer questions before a Senate subcommittee looking into communist influence in high schools. "Every intellectual who is called before one of the committees ought to refuse to testify," Einstein wrote. With Einstein's permission, that letter, too, was published, triggering another flood of hate mail and denunciations on the editorial pages of newspapers across the nation. And in 1953, when the enemies of Oppenheimer succeeded in stripping him of his security clearance because he had associated with Communist Party members before the war, Einstein mobilized faculty members at the institute to sign a petition in support of their director.

Einstein lived just long enough to see the flames of McCarthyism dying down. Senator McCarthy's career effectively ended when he was censured by the Senate in December 1954. But by that time Einstein was subsiding as well. Yet to the end, he was active in the struggle to prevent a nuclear war. One of his last public acts, in April 1955, was to sign a manifesto sent to him by his friend Bertrand Russell warning again about the dangers of nuclear weapons. It led to the establishment of the Pugwash Conferences on Science and World Affairs, which began in 1957 to bring scientists and thinkers together to address the problem of a nuclear armed world.

By the time Russell, back in London, received Einstein's signed version of the manifesto, Einstein was gone. On April 14, 1955, he collapsed at his home. The aneurysm discovered years earlier had begun to burst. When doctors suggested a last ditch attempt at surgery to repair the aorta, Einstein refused. "I have done my share," he told Dukas. "It is time to go. I will do it elegantly."

The following morning, overcome by pain, he was taken to the hospital, where even in his final days, he worked on calculations in his unflagging quest for a unified field theory. There were 12 pages of them by his bedside when he died, shortly after 1 a.m. on April 18.

In accordance with his wishes, Einstein was cremated that same day in Trenton, N.J. In attendance were Hans Albert, Dukas and a few old friends. His ashes were scattered along the nearby Delaware River. Weirdly, his brain was preserved. Dr. Thomas Harvey, the pathologist at Princeton Hospital who performed the routine autopsy took it upon himself to embalm Einstein's brain and keep it. The family was horrified, but Harvey convinced Hans Albert that there was scientific value in studying it. For the next 43 years, as he moved around the country with the brain always with him, Harvey would occasionally distribute slices to researchers.

Three scientific studies resulted in a handful of intriguing papers. One even determined that a part of the brain believed to play an important role in mathematical and spatial thinking was in his case larger than the norm. But no examination of Einstein's brain has ever shed much light on the sources of his genius, a gift as great as the mysteries of the universe that it penetrated.

Picture Credits